Dilemmas in Talent Development in the Middle Grades: Two Views

Dilemmas in Talent Development in the Middle Grades: Two Views

Paul S. George
and
Joseph S. Renzulli/Sally M. Reis

Edited by
Thomas O. Erb

National Middle School Association
Columbus, Ohio

National Middle School Association
2600 Corporate Exchange Drive, Suite 370
Columbus, Ohio 43231
Telephone (800) 528-NMSA

Copyright© 1997 by National Middle School Association.

The materials presented herein are the expressions of the authors and do not necessarily represent the policies of NMSA.

NMSA is a registered servicemark of National Middle School Association.

Printed in the United States of America

Sue Swaim, Executive Director
Jeff Ward, Assistant Executive Director, Business Services
John Lounsbury, Senior Editor
Edward Brazee, Associate Editor
Mary Mitchell, Copy Editor/Designer
Marcia Meade, Senior Publications Representative
ISBN: 1-56090-123-3   NMSA Stock Number: 1246

Library of Congress Cataloging-in-Publication Data
George, Paul S.
    Dilemmas in talent development in the middle grades: two views/
Paul S. George, Joseph S. Renzulli, Sally M. Reis; edited by Thomas
    O. Erb.
        p.   cm.
    Includes bibliographical references.
    ISBN 1-56090-123-3
    1. Gifted children--Education (Middle school)--United States.
    2. Middle schools--United States--Curricula. 3. School management
and organization--United States. I. Renzulli, Joseph S. II. Reis,
Sally M. III. Erb. Thomas Owen. IV. National Middle School
Association. V. Title.
LC3993.9.G46   1997
371.95'73--dc21   97-41503
                                                            CIP

Table of Contents

About the Authors

Paul S. George is a member of the faculty of the Department of Educational Leadership at the University of Florida. For the past twenty-five years, Dr. George has studied school organization and management, focusing on three particular areas: middle school education, instructional grouping, and Japanese education. Currently, Dr. George is investigating changes in the organization and management of the American high school.

Joseph S. Renzulli is the Neag Professor and Director of the National Research Center on the Gifted and Talented at the University of Connecticut. His most recent book, *Schools for Talent Development* (Creative Learning Press, 1994), describes a practical plan for infusing the know-how of gifted education into a total school improvement process.

Sally M Reis is an Associate Professor of Educational Psychology at the University of Connecticut where she also serves as a Principal Investigator for the National Research Center on the Gifted and Talented. She was a teacher for fifteen years, eleven of which were spent working with gifted students at the elementary, middle, and high school levels.

Serving as editor of this project was **Thomas O. Erb**, editor of the *Middle School Journal* and professor in the Department of Teaching and Leadership at the University of Kansas. Over the past thirty years he has been a teacher on middle grades interdisciplinary teams as well as a middle grades teacher educator. His writing has focused on teaming and curriculum and their relationship to talent development in the middle grades.

I

Developing Talents in the Middle Grades: The Debate Continues

Thomas O. Erb

The charge has been leveled at middle level schools that they tend to bore high ability students much of the time. In short, it is claimed, many of these students' academic needs are not being met. This is a wrenching charge for middle school people to take. The parent of two gifted children put it this way (National Training Program for Gifted Education, 1996):

> If that child is gifted and needs special services, then they [sic] should have it. I don't see it as an either/or. I don't see it as a reward. I see it as just serving the needs of the children, whatever those needs may be. (p. 48)

A talented math student offered this perspective (National Training Program for Gifted Education, 1996):

> If I were in a regular math class, not an advanced math class, I wouldn't feel challenged, because I need to be in the accelerated [one] because I've already learned all there is to [know] about the normal one. (p. 50)

How do middle school advocates reconcile their belief in the obligation to meet the needs of all young adolescents with the charge that high ability students are being shortchanged in the process of teaching all students in heterogeneous classes?

Even the shadow studies that have appeared in the middle school literature, lend support to the contention that middle school classrooms are generally boring, unchallenging places. Regular middle grades students, those not identified as gifted, were quoted in Lounsbury and Clark (1990) as describing their classes in these ways:

- Some were too easy. (p. 76)
- They are rather boring. (p. 86)
- I don't really feel challenged. (p. 98)

My preservice students who have examined the six shadow studies in Lounsbury and Clark (1990) were drawn to the conclusion that worksheets and teacher talk dominate the lives of eighth graders. With few exceptions, students have little student-to-student interaction. In fact, they have very little student-teacher interaction: Mostly teachers talk at students; there is little "connecting" going on in the majority of the classrooms depicted.

The exceptions to this dismal picture in the Lounsbury and Clark book, *Inside Grade Eight,* are a couple of shadow studies done on interdisciplinary teams where students were engaged in cooperative learning and frequent hands-on projects where they conversed with fellow students and teachers about their work.

Middle school classrooms are not supposed to be boring, disengaging places. They are to be characterized by integrated curriculum, or at least interdisciplinary curriculum, where students work at their own paces and at their own levels to produce projects that demonstrate meaningful applications of the knowledge they are acquiring. Students are supposed to be investigating the questions that they themselves are asking about the world and their place in it. They are supposed to be solving problems as they work in interdependent work groups. All of this effort is directed toward producing products and performances for some real audience. Yet we hear time and again that teachers just cannot meet these goals with all the diversity – developmental, academic, and emotional – of students that they encounter in their classrooms.

Since William Alexander (1965/1995) first described a new concept for a school in the middle, the need for middle schools has been justified on the grounds that young adolescents require educational programs that are developmentally appropriate. Whatever the needs of young adolescents are, there is little disagreement with Mead's (1965) observation that young adolescents are more unlike each other than they have ever been or will be again later in life. Developmental appropriateness has always been tempered with developmental diversity. In the physical domain, all five Tanner Stages are present in a typical middle level school. Cognitive development spans early concrete operations to solid formal operations. Social-emotional development spans the range from adult-pleasing preadolescents to emotionally mature young adults.

The developmental diversity is accompanied by other differences that have been shown to influence learning. Gender makes a difference, especially for girls in math and science. There are studies that have documented the advantages of single-sex classes in math and science to better meet the academic needs of girls (Streitmatter, 1997, under review). Ethnicity makes a difference. We can find in the literature examples of programs designed to meet the special needs of Black males (Gill, 1995). Certainly, ability, interest, and motivation make a difference in learning. These differences cut across different learners in different ways. For example, consider these two hypothetical, yet very real profiles of young adolescents: A late-concrete-operations, Tanner 3, emotionally mature, Black female, of average ability in math, and high motivation in English will have different needs than a full-formal operations, Tanner 1, preadolescent, Hispanic male, of average ability and motivation except for science where his ornithology projects win first place ribbons at the science fair. Of course, the various developmental characteristics of our two learners will be in a constant state of flux during the time that they are in the middle schools. Their other qualities will also wax and wane as new interests develop and old ones are sated.

For most of this century our solution to this diversity was to create new classes or programs to meet the needs of these diverse learners. Once the one-room schoolhouse was replaced by grade-leveled elementary schools and departmentalized high schools – both junior and senior – specializations grew exponentially to meet these needs. Subject specialization was followed by tracking, which was followed by categorical special education programs, which were followed by various title and chapter programs, which have recently been followed by at-risk programs. For whatever the need, we have a classroom designed to deal with it. Of course, we trip over our own organization when we attempt to deal with "multiply exceptional" youth. The gifted-in-math, learning-disabled, second-language-learner who lives with his adoptive parents who do not share his culture of origin gives us fits scheduling all the special classes designed to meet his needs. And meeting his needs in several separate classes is made all the more difficult by the fact that in most schools these classes are taught by educators who generally do not talk to each other.

The middle school movement has been at the forefront of the notion that students' complex needs are best met by bringing the services to the students rather than taking the students to the services. So instead of organizing the school around departments or specializations, middle schools are organized around interdisciplinary teams. In theory anyway, various specialists plan together on the interdisciplinary team to deliver academic services to the diverse set of students who comprise the learning community called a team or house.

However, we are hearing a loud cry that the system is not working for at least one subset of learners, those often labeled "gifted" or "high ability." Indeed, nearly one half of schools calling themselves middle schools do not even pretend to be using interdisciplinary teams (McEwin, Dickinson, & Jenkins, 1996). Many that do are at various stages of making them work effectively. For whatever reasons, we hear that many students are not challenged academically when they are placed on heterogeneously grouped teams.

To further complicate the discussion, the field of gifted education is undergoing some of the same types of changes that middle level education is undergoing. Whereas middle level education is moving away from departmentalization and tracking toward interdisciplinary teams, exploratory and integrated curriculum, and flexible scheduling and grouping, gifted education is moving away from the monolithic definition of gifted being scoring in the top 2% on an IQ or standardized achievement test toward definitions that include multiple characteristics across a variety of domains. Some of these domains may be broad while others are more specific (Gardner, 1983; Renzulli, 1994). The changing definitions of giftedness as advanced by Sternberg (1990), Tannenbaum (1986), Maker (1987), and Renzulli (1978, 1986) have been reviewed by Erb (1992; also see Sternberg & Davidson, 1986). What constitutes giftedness has been broadened considerably in recent years so that the concept takes in a larger number of young people in an increasing number of intellectual domains.

The debate about how to meet the needs of high ability learners in the context of a school designed to deliver diverse services to students heated up in the early 1990s. Paul George (1988), whose argument against tracking appeared in the *Middle School Journal,* has been at the center of this debate. He has launched a counter attack on advocates for special programs for gifted learners in the middle grades. In this volume, George continues to make the "legal brief" against these programs. Continuing with his prosecutorial stance, George argues that (a) gifted and talented youth can have their reasonable academic needs met in the context of regular classrooms, (b) special programs for gifted and talented youth are inequitable because they deprive other learners of their fair share of resources, and (c) many advocates for gifted and talented students misinterpret the evidence on ability grouping, middle schools, and gifted programs. He goes beyond a discussion of curriculum and instruction issues to target the political arena within which educational decisions are often made.

Two scholars who have led the movement to broaden the definition of giftedness respond with some proposals of their own for meeting the needs of above average youth who also show creativity and task commitment. Joseph Renzulli and Sally Reis discuss the changing views of giftedness. They go on to argue the case for curriculum differentiation and flexible grouping practices. Next they explain their

"Schoolwide Enrichment Model," which they see as compatible with the notion of exemplary middle schools. Along the way, they do not shrink from the challenge presented by Paul George. In fact, they accuse him of the very same "political" manipulation of evidence that he accuses advocates for the gifted of engaging in.

After the two sets of protagonists in this debate laid out their initial positions, they were each given the opportunity to respond to the other's opening chapter. George calls on middle school educators to redouble their efforts to deal with diverse learners in heterogeneous teams. He even professes an interest in the "Schoolwide Enrichment Model" espoused by Renzulli and Reis. However, he continues to warn that advocates for the gifted are playing into the hands of those who would dismantle our public schools.

Renzulli and Reis weigh the relative importance in educational decision-making of power and politics on the one hand and research on the other. They propose a "Me-as-researcher" model to strengthen the influence of research in this mix. What George views as "privilege" for the few, Renzulli and Reis characterize as "opportunity" for the deserving.

Whether you are a middle school advocate or an advocate for the gifted, you will not be able to read this volume without having an emotional as well as an intellectual reaction. This book is not a tepid attempt to patch over different views of how to develop the gifts and talents of middle school learners. Contained herein is a rich array of professional opinions that are advanced from different places on the landscape. National Middle School Association is pleased to offer our readers this thought-provoking exchange. Our hope is that a clearer view emerges about how educators can work together to provide the curricular and instructional differentiation necessary to challenge all learners and to do this without resorting to the hyperspecialization that proved so problematic in factory-model junior high schools characterized by departmentalization and IQ-based gifted programs. This work offers several ideas to help us move beyond the rigid categories of the past. ■

References

Alexander, W. M. (1995). The junior high school: A changing view. *Middle School Journal, 26* (3), 21-24. (Reprinted from *Readings in curriculum,* pp. 418-425, by G. Hass & K. Wiles, Eds., 1965, Boston: Allyn & Bacon).

Erb, T. O. (1992). Encouraging gifted performance in middle schools. *Midpoints Occasional Papers, 3* (1). Columbus, OH: National Middle School Association.

Gardner, H. (1983). *Frames of mind.* New York: Basic Books.

George, P. S. (1988). Tracking and ability grouping: Which way for the middle school? *Middle School Journal, 20* (1), 21-28.

Gill, W. (1995). Reversing the demise and preventing the apocalypse: Using alternative programs to help African American males. *Middle School Journal, 27* (2), 23-27.

Lounsbury, J. H., & Clark, D. C. (1990). *Inside grade eight: From apathy to excitement.* Reston, VA: National Association of Secondary School Principals.

Maker, C. J. (1987). Gifted and talented. In V. Richardson-Koehler (Ed.), *Educators' handbook: A research perspective* (pp. 420-456). New York: Longman.

McEwin, C. K., Dickinson, T. S., & Jenkins, D. M. (1996). *America's middle schools: Practices and progress—A 25 year perspective.* Columbus, OH: National Middle School Association.

Mead, M. (1965). Early adolescence in the United States. *Bulletin of the National Association of Secondary School Principals, 49* (300), 5-10.

National Training Program for Gifted Education. (1996). *Gifted education and middle schools.* Reston, VA: Council for Exceptional Children.

Renzulli, J. S. (1978). What makes giftedness? Reexamining a definition. *Phi Delta Kappan, 60,* 180-184, 261.

Renzulli, J. S. (1986). The three-ring conception of giftedness: A developmental model for creative productivity. In R. J. Sternberg & J. E. Davidson (Eds.), *Conceptions of giftedness* (pp. 53-92). New York: Cambridge University Press.

Renzulli, J. S. (1994). *Schools for talent development: A practical plan for total school improvement.* Mansfield Center, CT: Creative Learning Press.

Sternberg, R. J. (1990). What constitutes a "good" definition of giftedness? *Journal for the Education of the Gifted, 14,* 96-100.

Sternberg, R. J., & Davidson, J. E. (1986). *Conceptions of giftedness.* New York: Cambridge University Press.

Streitmatter, J. (1997). An exploratory study of risk-taking in a girls-only middle school math class. *Elementary Education Journal 98* (1), 15-26.

Streitmatter, J. (under review). Single-gender classes: Female physics students state their case. *School Science and Mathematics Journal.*   .

Tannenbaum, A. J. (1986). The enrichment matrix model. In J.S. Renzulli (Ed.), *Systems and models for developing programs for the gifted and talented* (pp. 391-428). Mansfield Center, CT: Creative Learning Press.

II

Middle Schools, Ability Grouping, and Gifted Students: The Continuing Conundrum

Paul S. George

Recent years have witnessed an unfortunately deep rift develop, and continue to widen, between advocates (both educators and parents) for the special needs of gifted students and other educators not directly associated with gifted education. These differences seem to be felt most sensitively at the middle school level. While this chapter may possibly contribute to the further estrangement of these groups, any lasting rapprochement between or among the parties involved cannot be permanently achieved by avoiding a full, open, and caring confrontation of the issues which divide the groups. Hence, what follows is intended to be just that – as complete a catalogue of criticisms and concerns about the current status of gifted education and the middle school as can be mustered, delivered in the belief that this sort of ventilation is an unpleasant but necessary part of the process of reconciliation.

These charges are proffered with the full knowledge that the reaction from many readers is likely to be lightning swift and largely negative. It is hoped that out of the interactions which will follow, heated though they may be, educators can arrive at a more accurate and informed understanding of the situation from a variety of perspectives that will ultimately lead to planning for schools that more fully meet the needs of all middle school students. If advocates for the gifted and those with other priorities are never able to engage in this sort of discussion, schools which respond to our leadership will rarely be able to put in place programs which effectively challenge, equitably, all students with learning experiences which prepare them for life in the community of tomorrow.

Let me attempt to state forthrightly my biases and my position at the outset. I believe that Dewey (1944) was correct when he argued that the way in which we organize and operate our schools determines to a large degree, or at least mirrors, the sort of communities we live in as adults. He was also correct, I think, when he suggested that what the best and wisest members of the community want for their own children must be what the community wants for all its children (Dewey, 1944). I believe that, in order to live together in peace and justice as citizens of communities, states, and the nation, we must work to ensure in all phases of our lives together, including middle school, that every member of those communities participates equally in the opportunities available. I believe that we must scrupulously avoid the extension of special privileges to any individual or group, in or out of school, because the existence of such privilege threatens the possibility that we will be able to live together anywhere, for long, in peace, harmony, unity, and fulfillment.

I believe that each of these concepts makes good sense: gifted education, ability grouping, and middle school. However, in the political and pedagogical rough and tumble of implementation of such concepts in the real world of public schools, what has too often emerged in practice has barely resembled the original ideas or intentions. When gifted education programs are organized and operated in ways which involve the unreasonable extension of special privileges to those involved, such programs must either be modified or dismantled. When advocates for gifted programs ignore the possibility of special privilege and continue to argue for the preservation and protection of such programs without regard for the school as a whole, they must be publicly challenged. Here, then, are the four propositions which I wish to propose for consideration. (Perhaps they may seem more like broadsides being fired indiscriminately. I want to acknowledge that, in terms of Myers-Briggs-type psychology, I am an extroverted feeling type. This means that I learn through active construction, and through interaction and response. I am certain that I have learned from writing this chapter and will learn from studying and responding to the reactions that follow it. These propositions and the supporting arguments are not finished; I expect to rethink and reformulate them in response to the discussion and dialogue that I hope will follow.)

1. There is no hard evidence to suggest that gifted and talented (GT) students cannot have virtually all of their reasonable academic needs met in the context of the regular classroom. The continued denigration of the regular classroom by advocates for the gifted, in an effort to secure isolated classes and programs for GT students, has resulted in a growing lack of public confidence about the quality of their schools.

2. The implementation of GT programs frequently involves the extension of special learning privileges to these students, depriving the others of their proper share of the resources that the school has to offer.

3. In their eagerness to establish effective programs, some advocates for gifted and talented students have been guilty of less than professional activity in their interpretation of the evidence on middle schools, gifted programs, ability grouping, related issues, and the recommendations which they issue for school programs related to that research.

4. Educators have more urgent concerns which require the concerted energy and commitment of all of us.

PROPOSITION ONE
There is no hard evidence to suggest that gifted and talented (GT)students cannot have virtually all of their reasonable academic needs met in the context of the regular classroom.

Academic achievement in our schools

Regular classrooms in American schools are as good as or better than they have ever been. The continued denigration of the regular classroom by advocates of the gifted as unfit for their students is not based on fact, and is an unprofessional disservice to American public education. Ironically, the harsh criticism of the regular classroom will contribute to the growing general public disaffection with the public schools in a way that also eventually damages programs for gifted and talented students. It is in the interest of all students for educators of the gifted to join in support, rather than condemnation, of public school education.

Consider some of the now established facts of academic achievement in American public schools, including the middle level, revealed by reviewers of research such as Gerald Bracey and the once secret, now well-known, federal government's Sandia National Laboratory Report. (Charged by the Bush administration to investigate achievement in American public schools, the researchers at Sandia National Laboratories turned in a careful, scholarly analysis of the evidence. The report, full of good news about American schools, was the exact opposite of what the Bush administration wanted to hear, so publication and discussion of the report was forbidden by our national government.) Among the conclusions now readily available to the public as a result of the discovery and eventual publication of that report (Carson, Huelskamp, & Woodall, 1992) are these:

1. Only one in 20 American business people is critical of the academic skills of their workers. American business people are much more concerned about the social skills of their employees than their academic skills, the same social skills that middle school educators have striven to develop through advisory programs and team organization.
2. American students are near the top in reading on international comparison tests (Bracey, 1993a).
3. American public schools, and the post-secondary education that follows, actually produce more mathematicians and scientists than needed (Carson, Huelskamp, & Woodall, 1992).

4. Performance on standardized tests (like the SAT and the GRE) has been steady or improving for the last 20 years. Since the early 1970s, scores on most standardized tests have been steady or rising, with scores on some of these tests standing at a 30-year high. This is true for the SAT, NAEP, PSAT, MAT, CTBS, GRE, LSAT, and for IQ tests. It is also true of the College Board's Advanced Placement tests and the SAT Achievement Tests.

There is no evidence whatsoever of a decline in test scores in American schools, yet advocates of the gifted often claim that the regular classroom has become such a poor learning environment that GT students should be withdrawn and isolated from the general population of the schools. Such programs proliferate in American school districts on the assumption that the regular classroom is no longer suitable for GT students.

According to the *Sandia Report* (Carson, Huelskamp, & Woodall, 1992), scores of students compared by their class rank have remained fairly steady since 1975, about the time middle schools were being established in large numbers. Back in 1975 most of the students who took the SAT were white males, from the middle and upper middle class, who were in the top 20% of their high school graduating class. If you consider only the scores of the typical students who took the SAT in 1975 (white, male, upper middle class), compared to the same type of student today, scores have increased for this group by about 40 points, more than 10 percentile ranks! If you look at how these students are doing today, the answer is "Much better!" As Berliner (1993) described it:

> Among these advantaged, primarily white youths, who were supposedly achieving less because they suffered from harmful desegregation policies, low standards of performance, poor teachers, no homework, too much television, low morals, and a host of other plagues, we find considerable improvement in performance on the SAT. (p. 635)

The National Assessment of Educational Progress, called "our nation's report card," is given to students who are 9, 13, and 17 years old. It covers six areas: mathematics, science, reading, writing, geography, and computer skills. The results of these tests have remained steady for 20 years, with African Americans and Hispanics improving steadily. White students have also improved slightly. Test scores have also been steady when you look at where the schools are, even in what are called the "disadvantaged metro" schools. The government report (Carson, Huelskamp, & Woodall, 1992) says that "If anything, today's students are performing better than previous students" (p. 271). Scores in the basic skills areas have also been maintained without damaging the scores in advanced skills like critical thinking.

One group of scientists reviewing the results of NAEP tests concluded that "the national data on student performance do not indicate a decline in *any* area" (Berliner, 1993, p. 635). This is even clearer when you realize that they have been making the tests more difficult (by "renorming") all along. Berliner likens it to a high jump contest, with someone setting the bar higher and higher all the time. Thinking of it this way, he says, means that about 85% of today's students are doing better on tests than the average parent did! Berliner says that if we gave our students tests on "decoding information from complex audiovisual presentations" or "comprehending extremely fast-changing video arrays of information," our students would look much smarter. How about a test on how to program your VCR? Who would do best there, our middle school students or us?

This lack of decline is also true of other major standardized tests, like the Stanford Achievement Test, the Metropolitan Achievement Test (MAT), and the Comprehensive Test of Basic Skills (CTBS), as well as the Advanced Placement (AP) Tests. Students take the AP tests to get college credit while still in high school. In the last two decades the number of students attempting them has increased by 500%, including many poor and minority students. During this time, the number of Asians taking AP tests has tripled, the percentage of African Americans taking the tests has doubled, and the percentage of

14

Hispanics has quadrupled. In spite of all these new test-takers and the deteriorating social conditions from which they come, the scores on AP tests have remained relatively stable for the last two decades, declining 11/100s of one point since 1978 (Hodgkinson, 1993). We certainly cannot explain this by saying the middle and high schools are failing!

The scores of our top students have not suffered either. For example, the College Board's Achievement Tests are taken only by 8% of the students. Scores on these tests have increased since 1979, right along with rising SAT scores for the same top students (Hodgkinson, 1993). This is even true of the very best students, those who go on to college and then decide to pursue a graduate degree like a masters or doctorate. The Graduate Record Exam (GRE) is the test required for entrance to the best graduate schools in American universities. These top students score as well on the verbal portion as top students did 20 years ago, and in mathematics the scores are much higher. From 1980 to 1990 the scores on the GRE verbal increased 16 points and mathematics produced a 36-point improvement. These sorts of scores are also true in the field of law (LSAT) and medicine (MCAT). The quality of our scientists, lawyers, and physicians has been increasing for the last decade. Berliner (1993) concluded more students are taking the tests, more are getting college degrees, and they have also learned a great deal more.

There is no convincing evidence that students in American schools do poorly in comparison to students in other countries. It is common sense, really. As others have pointed out, it would be impossible for American middle and high schools to be so bad on tests of mathematics and science and still have the United States lead the world in these areas. And the United States does lead the world. Americans have won more Nobel prizes than all of the rest of the world put together. Americans dominate the world in scientific publications, patents, and awards. In fact, 40% of the scientific articles in the world are published by American scholars; no other nation produces more than 7% (Bracey, 1993b).

Bracey (1993a) also pointed out that American students are, and have been, near the top in reading. In fact, in the Second International Assessment of Educational Progress, our children were second in reading out of 32 nations. In addition, our children's reading performance has been remarkably steady throughout the entire 20th century. Why do we do so much better in reading than we do in math? Because we care more about it and work harder to teach and learn it .

Recent investigations (Carson, Huelskamp, & Woodall, 1992) of international comparisons of academic achievement reveal that such studies may be very misleading. It seems, for example, that America tests all of its students and other countries may include only their very best. Hong Kong may get first place in math, for example, but some scholars believe that the tested population includes only 3% of Hong Kong's 12th graders who take math. Many countries only test students from their best schools (Bracey, 1991).

There is reason to believe that the Ministry of Education in Japan "manipulates the test scores" so that only scores of students from top schools are reported (George, 1995). In Japan, only the best 1/3 of the students even go to college preparatory public high schools; the rest go to commercial and vocational high schools. No attempts are made to insure that each participating country takes a scientifically representative sample of its student population. No attempts are made to adjust for ethnic or socioeconomic differences in tested groups. The fact is that the international tests compare incomparable populations. When America's top 10% is compared to the top 10% of the students from the highest performing countries, our test scores are every bit as high.

American schools also teach different subjects at different grade levels than they are taught in other countries. If Algebra I and Geometry are on the test for 13-year-olds, and American schools teach algebra primarily in the 9th grade and geometry in the 10th grade, that means our middle school students are being tested on subjects they have not yet been taught. If we looked at our eighth grade algebra students, compared to Japanese eighth grade algebra students, I believe we would find that there would be very few differences in achievement.

If you are a parent, and are still concerned about what international comparisons say about the value of the regular classroom experience for gifted learners, ask yourself whether you would want to subject your children to the life-style of the Indian, Korean, or Japanese child in order to achieve a few more points on a test score. The typical Japanese middle level student goes to school up to 60 days more a year, for up to an hour longer each day. A great majority of Japanese students also attend private "cram" schools several evenings each week for the entire 12 years they are in school. The pressure and stress in the lives of Japanese children is incredibly intense and uniformly condemned around the world (George, 1995).

A Japanese parent was recently asked, "When do your children play?" His response was "Play? Japanese children do not play." In many ways, these children do not have the type of balanced childhood and youth that most American parents want for their own children. Our students would have to have very different childhoods in order to score a few points higher on comparison tests. Remember that Berliner (1993) points out that our students are known around the world as creative, spontaneous, and critical thinkers; and they go on to do very challenging work in college, in numbers that are the envy of the rest of the world. Our system is not worse. It is organized and operated differently and in many ways is equal to or better than other school systems around the world.

As a matter of fact, the Japanese reject the concept of giftedness and adamantly refuse to organize isolated classes for such students (George, 1989). Japan, to which advocates of the gifted point as an exemplar of the kind of achievement which ought to typify our own schools, practices the very sort of heterogeneous grouping the advocates seek to discredit. Effort, not ability, is the explanation of achievement in Japan.

In face of all of these facts, respected advocates for the gifted choose to select and identify with the most negative characterizations of academic achievement in the public school classroom (e.g., Feldhusen, 1991, 1992; Gallagher, 1988, 1991). "Our vaunted economic superiority over other nations is rapidly disappearing," wrote Gallagher (1988, p. 107), suggesting that the decline was due to the failure of the regular classroom in the public school. Assuming, and broadcasting, the worst about the regular classroom, Gallagher (1991) later stated that "Good seed needs good soil in order to flourish intellectually" (p. 13). The implication seems clear – that the students left behind in the regular classroom are the "bad seed" deserving only "bad soil" in which to live out their blighted intellectual potential. I believe that this sort of broadside is a terribly destructive disservice to schools, children, their parents and teachers – indeed to all Americans.

Challenging the gifted in the regular classroom

If the research makes it clear that academic achievement in American public school classrooms is not declining, it is also true that recent developments in curriculum and instruction also make separation of the gifted and talented much less necessary than advocates for isolated programs argue. Instructional strategies such as cooperative learning, mastery learning, curriculum compacting, co-teaching, reading-writing workshops, whole language, interdisciplinary curriculum, and higher order thinking strategies have been researched carefully and to the point that there should be little question as to their efficacy (Reis, 1994; Slavin, 1990b, 1991). We can be confident that we know a great deal more about how to individualize instruction and differentiate the curriculum than ever before. For example, a great deal of work in the technique called curriculum compacting indicates that it is possible to eliminate 24% to 75% of the repetitive curriculum in three hours of staff development (Reis & Purcell, 1993). If 75% of the repetitive curriculum can be eliminated in as little as three hours of training (Reis, 1994), why is it necessary to permanently remove and isolate gifted and talented students in rigid ability groups?

Recent research from the National Research Center for Gifted and Talented supports the contention that gifted youth can be challenged in the regular classroom. In the *Newsletter*, Archambault, Westberg, and Brown (1992) reported on a study that identified a large number of techniques that could be used with gifted and talented students in the regular classroom: advanced readings, independent projects, enrichment worksheets, extended reports, elimination of previously mastered curriculum through pretesting, opportunities for more advanced level work, involvement in decisions regarding classroom time allocation, exposure to higher level thinking skills, working in locations other than the classroom, enrichment centers, opportunities to pursue self-selected interests, work in groups with common interests, moving to a higher grade for specific subject area instruction, working with students of comparable ability across classrooms at the same grade level, working on an advanced or enriched curriculum unit on a teacher-selected topic, participating in a competitive program focusing on thinking skills or problem solving, and receiving concentrated instruction in critical thinking and creative problem solving. None of these techniques seems more complex than curriculum compacting, which can apparently be done well after three hours of training. There are obviously, then, many techniques which, if used effectively, would make it unnecessary to remove GT students from the regular classroom. Why are the advocates of the gifted not clamoring for the opportunity to help make this happen?

What is the likelihood of such practices being used with gifted students in the regular classroom? Indeed, the evidence does seem to indicate that such practices are all too rarely used and that too often these students are faced with stultifyingly undifferentiated curriculum and dullingly standard instruction. The result for gifted students, we are often told, is "crashing boredom." Crashing boredom is not, however frequently it may be claimed, the exclusive burden of the gifted student. Some advocates for GT students continue to imply that because GT students are bored, they are more deserving of the school's best instruction than are other students, and should, therefore, be removed from classrooms with mediocre teachers to separate classrooms.

The existence of isolated programs for gifted and talented students may also be contrary to other important goals of middle school programs and of good education in general (Sapon-Shevin, 1994). Core programs essential to the effectiveness of entire middle schools, such as the interdisciplinary team, block scheduling, advisory programs, and others, may be made more difficult by the restrictive schedules required to provide a separate program for gifted students. The perceived needs of 5% of the students in a school should not, however, be the driving force in the organization and operation of the school as a whole, whether these students are a part of marching band, GT programs, or some other small group.

Such programs may also have, as by-products, negative outcomes for the self-esteem of many other learners. At least they may offer privileged self-esteem boosting opportunities to some and deny them to others, simply from the very act of grouping. The most recent large scale research on ability grouping and self-esteem (Power, 1994), using data from 18,000 students, suggests that self-affirming experiences are more readily available in high tracks and that students in low tracks may suffer comparatively. Are we willing to take chances with more than a million students while we wait to evaluate additional research?

PROPOSITION TWO

The implementation of GT programs frequently in-volves special grouping arrangements which provide GT students with learning privileges which are denied to the other middle school students, depriving these students of their proper share of the resources that the school has to offer.

By 1994 in virtually every state the average school district was becoming more and more desperate financially. When there are only the most meager funds for curriculum enrichment on a schoolwide basis, no group should retain special opportunities for field trips, for the use of computers, for bringing in visitors, or for monies required for materials for special enrichment curriculum units. When gifted and talented programs, as they are offered in many schools, boil down to primarily curriculum enrichment opportunities, and not acceleration, there seems to be little justification for their existence. When enrichment programs serve a small percentage of the students in a school, when the activities are often not those mandated by the state, and when other students do not experience such enrichment, unwarranted special privilege exists (Sapon-Shevin, 1994).

A substantial part of the disagreement between advocates for the gifted and their challengers centers on whether ability grouping and other programs which bring gifted and talented students together in separate and often isolated classes actually produce higher academic achievement as measured by standardized tests. The conclusions one draws about the issue of whether ability grouping is beneficial to the academic achievement of gifted students and others seem to be highly correlated with which portion of the research one reads, which researchers one respects, and the groups of students for which one is an advocate.

I believe, after reading analyses of the research by Slavin (1987, 1990a, 1993), Noland & Taylor (1986), Oakes (1985, 1990), Gamoran & Berends (1987), Rogers (1991), Kulik (1992), and Kulik & Kulik (1984,1991), that except for situations in which a group or class of students receive, through special privilege, the very best learning situations a middle school can offer, ability grouping fails to deliver increased academic achievement. It seems reasonable to conclude that when grouping does seem to deliver higher achievement to one group, that it does so through a sort of zero sum game where students who are not in the top group suffer further from having certain school resources denied to them. Slavin (1993) concluded that ability grouping had little or no effect on achievement in middle level schools and that, indeed, all forms of grouping are equally ineffective, in all subjects.

I am convinced by the experiences I have had in hundreds of middle schools over the last three decades that educational resources are not always – not even frequently, in fact, rarely – distributed equitably in terms of what gifted students receive compared to what all other learners have available for their learning. My experience tells me that this is because the process of assigning the school's resources for learning to different groups of students can often be as much a political decision as it is a pedagogical one. Compared to the so-called average or standard classes, class sizes of advanced (and remedial sections) seem, in many middle level schools, to be much smaller. The status attached to membership in these different class groups is incontestably highest in the advanced groups and lowest in basic and remedial sections; no student, certainly no parent, publicly boasts about placement into remedial classes. By contrast, consider the supercilious manner of some parents of gifted students.

Does anyone question that in the advanced classes, time on task is most certainly much higher and a positive climate for learning, with appropriately high expectations for success, is clearly more likely to be in place (Page, 1991)? One need only recall the TV situation comedy featuring the "Sweat Hogs" to realize how difficult teaching becomes when the class represents a "critical mass of discouragement." It is, of course, highly unlikely that such a classroom could be an effective learning environment. That such a situation, making fun of discouraged learners, could become a highly successful comedy is sad indeed. The answer to such situations, if equity is something we really care about, does not lie in removing the gifted students to some instructional haven safely isolated from the rest of the school world. It seems clear to me that it is folly to hope that there can long be isolated islands of calm and plenty in a sea of discouragement and denial, in or out of school.

The essential inequity of ability grouping as it is often practiced may extend to the way in which teachers are assigned to classes grouped in various ways. Assigning teachers, it seems, may also be as much a political process in many schools as it is a pedagogical one. In educational organizations, with few levels of professional advancement available, assignment to teaching the students one prefers is one of the few career incentives which principals can use to reward the more successful and experienced teachers on a staff (Darling-Hammond, 1995). Both evidence and experience suggest that teachers strongly prefer to teach advanced classes. In one study only 3% of the teachers expressed an interest in teaching the low ability groups (Findley and Bryan, 1975). Charged with maintaining the motivation of the teaching staff, many middle school principals assign the most successful teachers to teaching the most successful students, and the least successful (or unproved and inexperienced) staff members are assigned to the students who have had the most difficulty learning.

This is sometimes combined with pressure on the principal to pacify politically powerful or otherwise influential parents. In many school districts it appears that an unspoken obligation of the middle school principal is to keep angry parents away from the central office. Too many angry, influential parents pounding on the superintendent's door can often develop into a career-limiting situation for school administrators. So, when certain parents request that their students have specific teachers, principals may be receptive.

In defense of middle school principals, this may also be the case simply because these parents understand the difference one teacher can make, because they have the time to make the request, and because they are not intimidated about contacting the school principal to make such a request. Recent research has documented the highly effective advocacy brought to bear by parents of GT students and its absence in the lives of poor and minority students (Sapon-Shevin, 1994; Useem, 1992). It may be that most school principals respond positively and helpfully to all requests, even those of poor and minority group parents when they make them. However, the facts seem to be that, for whatever reason, middle school students perceived as having less potential for successful learning are often grouped together with teachers who have not established a record of success in teaching.

Well-known advocates for the gifted (e.g., Gallagher, 1991; Sicola, 1990) have ridiculed the suggestion that pressure from the parents of gifted and talented students is a significant factor in the organization and operation of programs to serve these students. Site-based management – in which teachers, administrators, and possibly many parents may have increasing control over decisions about grouping – has been regarded as a questionable practice, to be judged on the "results." The idea that personal and social concerns of young adolescents might be valued, along with intellectual interests, has been mocked.

Innovative, state-of-the-art instruction is sometimes distributed inequitably among classes with different ability groups. High ability, high achieving students are often perceived by teachers as receptive to unusual and creative teaching techniques; teachers believe that they can take instructional risks with such students because classroom behavior management is not a problem. Discouraged learners make teaching difficult, and high-risk strategies may be discarded in favor of learning methods which keep students still and quiet, lest things get out of control (Cooper, 1979).

Any teaching technique which threatens to detract from the advantages of advanced students is subject to incredibly negative invective from advocates for these already privileged students. In spite of what is to me an amazing array of evidence to the contrary, advocates for the gifted continue to attack cooperative learning. Gallagher (1991) referred to it as the "educational equivalent of using a screwdriver as a chisel" (p. 15). Sicola (1990) claimed that using gifted students in cooperative learning situations with other learners is "exploitation" of the meanest sort. After all, Sicola (1990) offered, "As far as intellectual, academic ability, creativity, and leadership are concerned...human beings are not created equally" (p. 41). The solution, Sicola suggested, is "flexible grouping" in which gifted students should receive all of their academic work in specially identified, isolated classes. Then they could be grouped heterogeneously with the other students in advisory programs, exploratory courses, and intramurals. This, it seems to me, is what advocates for the gifted often mean by "flexible grouping."

It also seems clear to me that middle school students in advanced classes are exposed to a much more enriched curriculum than students in other sections of the same course. The books are different. The assignments are different. The richness and robustness of classroom discussions are significantly different. Students in advanced classes are perceived as being "able to handle it." Oakes (1988) summarized the evidence:

It appears, however, that only the most extraordinary average and low-level classes match the curriculum standards, learning opportunities, and classroom climates of even ordinary high-track classes. (p. 43)

Discouraged students grouped together in low-track classes resent their status, respond defensively, and refuse to engage in the very academic efforts which might bring them more success. Teachers, accurately perceiving the student negativity and hostility, frequently respond in ways that actually increase the force of those factors. Good and Brophy (1987) concluded:

Even if teachers assigned to low-track classes do not have undesirable attitudes and expectations, they will find it difficult to establish effective learning environments in these classes because of the defeatism, alienation, and flat-out resistance they are likely to encounter there. (p. 407)

Oakes (1985) made it clear that the "hidden" aspects of the curriculum are also distributed unfairly. The implicit curriculum in advanced classes often seemed to be a curriculum of taking control, of leadership, of learning to be more active, of learning to take charge of their learning lives, of exercising choice, of managing their own learning so that they would learn to manage themselves and, later, others. By contrast, the experiences of students in basic classes seemed to be focused on learning to be more passive; to give up control of one's life; and to be quiet, punctual, clean, and orderly. The hidden curriculum in the lower tracks seemed ideal for preparing students for minimum wage labor opportunities, for being receptive to supervision and even, sadly, incarceration (Rosenbaum, 1976).

When advanced students are grouped together for acceleration, especially in mathematics, and provided with the best teachers, the best classroom learning climate, the most enriched curriculum, state-of-the-art instruction, and learning resources (e.g., computers), they learn more than they otherwise would. Who would not? Under these circumstances it seems clear, at least to me, that it is not the act of grouping which delivers the benefits, but the resources devoted to the achievement of a particular group.

PROPOSITION THREE

In their eagerness to establish effective programs, some advocates for gifted and talented students have been guilty of less than professional activity in their interpretation of the evidence on middle schools, gifted programs, ability grouping, and related issues, and the recommendations which they issue for school programs related to that research.

At least a few advocates for the gifted who have written about ability grouping, middle schools, and related topics seem uninformed about a variety of important issues, premature in their conclusions and recommendations, and unconcerned about anything but the narrow academic achievement of the smallest and already most privileged group of students in the school. Though this is certainly not true of all, or even the majority of writers who are advocates for the education of gifted and talented students, some of the most widely circulated of such writings are, in my judgment, guilty of these charges. Unfortunately, it seems that these writers have an influence on parents and practitioners that far exceeds their number. Let me illustrate.

If you read the works of some writers (e.g., Allen, 1991; Robinson, 1990; Rogers, 1991; Sicola, 1990) arguing strenuously against the middle school concept, condemning cooperative learning and heterogeneous grouping, or other related practices, you will almost always find that certain conditions prevail. Chief among these characteristics is what seems to me to be a myopic view of the process of schooling. Rarely in their writing do these authors indicate that they care for any but the small group of students in gifted and talented programs they prize so highly.

Many advocates for gifted students have failed to address the larger pressing needs of the school or the community. Said Lederer

(1992), program director for a GT program in Oregon, "We have been isolated and self-involved" (p. 34). Whether the school, as a whole, is successful for the hundreds of students who learn there does not seem to be something some advocates of the gifted care about.

Further, there seems to be little obvious concern for, or interest in, the changing demographics of our schools or of gifted programs. Advocates for the gifted, charged Lederer (1992), may study the "gifted underachiever" but ignore the "at risk" or "socially/emotionally disturbed" even though they know intuitively that these are often the same students. Wrote Lederer:

> They know that materials and techniques that have been
> developed for gifted and talented programs can be very
> effective when used in "alternative ed" programs but rarely
> press to include these students, especially if they have not
> been formally identified as gifted. Insofar as the numbers
> of African-Americans, Latino, and other minority students
> identified as gifted remain statistically low, the criticism of
> elitism is well-founded. Efforts at resolving this problem
> have been late, and few, and largely weak. (p. 34)

Surely we can agree that, at least until recently, relatively few articles on gifted education have addressed minority group concerns and that minorities are underrepresented in gifted programs at the middle school level even if the programs are "open."

These same advocates rarely, if ever, mention important social priorities that might be compromised by unrestrained concern with the needs of gifted and talented students: such as school district desegregation and within-school integration, the eradication of racism in education, the diminution of poverty and its differential effects on schooling, stopping the disintegration of the cities, development of a sense of community and unity in and out of school, or the relationship of these issues to the education of gifted and talented students. It is as if there was no obligation on the part of educators for the gifted to be concerned about the school as a whole, no responsibility for the larger group, only concern about whether or not the research says programs for the gifted produce higher scores on standardized tests for these students.

Words like *duty, responsibility, obligation, community, balance, fairness, unity, ownership, citizenship, teamwork,* and *sacrifice* are rarely if ever used in the public debate by the advocates for the needs of the gifted. I am not arguing that gifted programs are the cause of all of the problems in the school or the society; I am arguing that these students and their advocates have as much civic responsibility as everyone else and the moral obligation to be concerned as much about the school as a whole as they are about their students' placement in Ivy League universities.

In discussions of ability grouping, advocates rarely, if ever, mention any of the following: the incredible and rarely contested difficulties of identification and placement; the pervasive and recognizable "locked-in" factor; the importance of effort; problems with self-esteem which may result from inappropriate or inflexible placement; the real reason for any differences in achievement if and when they appear in reviews of research (which, I argue, is the unfair and inequitable distribution of teaching talent and other school resources); or the politics of gifted advocacy and the effects on school programs of the intervention of influential outsiders on school board and building level decisions. Few of these are mentioned in the literature of gifted education, except in attempts at denial or refutation.

At least a few advocates for GT programs accuse their opponents of ideology, while they practice it, or tolerate it, themselves. Sicola (1990), for example, referred continuously to middle school advocates as "philosophers" in what can only be a pejorative sense. Would she choose to identify her colleagues in gifted education as "philosophers"? Some among the advocates for the gifted copy and circulate copies of newsletters like the *Blumenfeld Education Letter.* In one copy of this letter, the author accused advocates of whole language of a "socialist agenda" (Blumenfeld, 1991a), and of wanting to change America into a "collectivist" society. The article maintained that whole language leads to reading disabilities and dyslexia. The June 1991 issue of that newsletter asserted that progressives "took over American education at the turn of the century," and that control continues:

> Obviously, there exists within the American education establishment a network of '60s leftists – well versed in the writings of Paolo Freire and John Dewey and other radical educators – who are now so well organized and entrenched in positions of power and influence throughout the university system, that they can virtually dictate how reading is to be taught in just about every primary school in America. And that is why we strongly urge parents to remove their children from the public schools and either teach them at home or put them in good private schools. (Blumenfeld, 1991b, p. 5)

The implication of having such charges uncritically circulated among parents of the gifted is that leftist egalitarians are out to secretly take over the schools and wrest a quality education away from their children. Circulating such inaccuracies is irresponsible; allowing them to be circulated, without strenuous disavowal, in support of special programs for the gifted is unprofessional. I have come to believe that advocacy for the gifted has unwittingly played into the hands of ultraconservative political groups that seem bent on the destruction of the public school system through choice, vouchers, and assorted other challenges (e.g., prayer in the school). Where are the vigorous denials, from advocates of the gifted, of such extreme views circulated on their behalf?

A very few on the fringe of these debates issue inaccurate generalizations about the decline of American education in order to justify the removal of gifted and talented learners from the mainstream regular classroom to support the creation of privileged, miniature private academies within the public schools (e.g., Sicola, 1990). They ignore all of the research cited above. For example, take an article widely circulated among supporters of programs for the gifted written by Singal

(1991), in *The Atlantic Monthly* . Singal recommended the following as solutions to the quagmire in which he believes education finds itself:

1. Dramatically increase the quality and quantity of assigned reading. By the senior year, college bound students should be reading the equivalent of 12 books a year for class, not counting textbooks, along with six to eight additional books in independent study and summer reading. Singal says that this sort of reading load was standard in our best schools a quarter century ago. (*In which classes? Of course, no references support these assertions.*)
2. Bring back survey courses in history and literature. [*As if they ever left.*]
3. Institute flexible ability grouping in elementary and secondary schools. (*Who disagrees?*)
4. Attract more bright college graduates into teaching, and abolish education courses since they spend too much time on Mickey Mouse issues. (*Like the ones which might prepare regular classroom teachers to challenge the gifted in the heterogeneous classroom?*)

Singal wrote (in apparent ignorance of the research arising from the *Sandia Report*) that the few schools that have kept test scores stable or even rising share two characteristics: academics receive priority over every other activity; these schools "require semester or year long courses in literature and encourage rigorous math classes, including geometry and advanced algebra" (p. 66). I wager that 99% of American high schools include all of these recommendations in their curriculum today. On what planet was this research conducted?

In support of these recommendations (which I believe would do nothing to improve American middle schools), Singal asserted that there has been a sharp decline in academic achievement and college entrance exam scores. Rebuttals to this sort of poorly documented argument deserve to be a part of the discussion about whether American schools have declined to the point that providing quasi-private academies within the public schools is the best way to respond to the thinly-veiled threat that all of these students will otherwise be enrolled in the first generation of Chris Whittle's private schools. The writing of Bracey (1991, 1992, 1993b, 1993c), Males (1992), and Berliner (1993) are just a few of the data-based, well-reasoned resources, along with the objective, Bush-administration-commissioned *Sandia Laboratory Report* (Carson, Huelskamp, & Woodall, 1992), which make it clear that American schools are as good, if not better, than they have ever been. This is so, the facts make clear, even if your focus is only on the segregated, all-white, upper middle class portion of the public schools that existed prior to school desegregation. Is a return to the schools of the past what advocates of the gifted really long for? Even a critic such as myself does not believe that the majority of advocates for gifted children would value such an option. However, popular but escapist comparisons to a romanticized past do little to help us face today's educational problems.

Some among the advocates of the gifted broadcast their own conclusions and recommendations about research on ability grouping and practices appropriate for education of the gifted as if these conclusions were finally established and unimpeachable fact (e.g., Rogers, 1991; Sicola, 1990). Reviews of research on ability grouping which conclude that ability grouping is good for the gifted and does little or no harm to other students seem to be, curiously, always conducted by advocates for the gifted or by those commissioned to do the reviews by editors of journals or associations for the gifted (e.g., Kulik, 1992). These reviews inevitably conclude, sometimes with incredible finality, that research says that ability grouping works, especially for the gifted student and that gifted students should, based on research findings, spend a majority of their day with others of similar abilities and interests. Which similar abilities? In Florida students are gifted if they have an IQ of 130. Is a score of 129 similar? Not in Florida. Do advocates of the gifted share any of the responsibility for improving such identification procedures? Fortunately, a few (e.g., Renzulli, 1994) have recently begun to acknowledge such a responsibility, but most never mention it.

Some advocates for the gifted conclude, from their reviews of the research (e.g., Allen, 1991), that cooperative learning should be used only sparingly with gifted and talented students, perhaps only for social skills development; and they imply that research has revealed this as the truth, once and for all. These writers use the phrase "supported by research" so often that they clearly wish to persuade readers that their positions, and their positions only, are obviously and unambiguously supported by research and others are just as obviously not. They do so through selective but numerous citations of studies and reviews that support only their point of view; as if the sheer number of citations was more important than logic, accuracy, balance, and fairness. Most of the research cited in these reviews is, by the way, about a quarter of a century old, reflecting a time when the demographics of the American school were very, very different. It appears that these writers assume that if they repeat these biased conclusions often enough, if they copy and distribute brief and skewed summaries of the research to enough parents of the gifted, that they will somehow "win" the debate.

Some writers and journal editors in the field of gifted education frequently dismiss or ignore the work of other writers and reviewers unless they are actively condemning it. The works of highly regarded and recognized researchers such as Oakes (1985, 1990), Gamoran, Nystroud, Berends, and LePore (1995), Rosenbaum (1976), Stevenson and Lee (1990), Joyce (1991), Slavin (1990b, 1991, 1993), and others who are harshly critical of ability grouping and question the favoritism they believe is often received by the gifted, are rarely examined in any detail unless it is done dismissively.

Some of the more extremist advocates for the gifted, instead, set up "straw man" arguments that the most inexperienced freshman debater would recognize as illogical. One publication (Fiedler-Brand, Lange, & Winebrenner, 1990) for example, used a "myth and reality" approach that was, in my opinion, an abuse of the principles of rea-soned dialogue. In this publication, the authors dismissed even the remote possibility that there might be validity to the charges that:
1. tracking and ability grouping are the same;
2. ability grouping could be elitist;

3. there could be any unfair discrimination against racial or ethnic minority students in the way gifted programs are operated;
4. gifted students could make it on their own in the regular classroom;
5. the way gifted programs operate might ever cause the self-esteem of others to suffer;
6. whole language approaches have merit and;
7. heterogeneously grouped cooperative learning could be effective with gifted students.

This particular publication even went so far as to say "it is possible that the students who may actually learn the LEAST [emphasis in original] in a given class are the gifted" (p. 5). This publication appears to have been designed for and received broad distribution among parents of the gifted.

I suggest that, in their writing, these and other authors who are advocates for the gifted almost always focus on only one important educational outcome (academic achievement of the gifted as measured on standardized tests), ignoring other terribly pressing needs on the broader educational agenda: schoolwide academic achievement, self-esteem, self-efficacy, effort, motivation, interpersonal communications, teamwork, problem solving, critical thinking, or any educational objectives that encompass all the learners in the school. I believe educators, as a group, would be more responsive to the needs of the gifted, if the advocates for these programs would indicate that they cared about the school as a whole and all the students in it.

PROPOSITION FOUR
Educators have more urgent concerns which require the concerted energy and commitment of all of us.

The United States Constitution leaves the conduct of education to the individual states. In most of these states, it is likely that the state constitution describes the education obligation of the state much as it does in my own state of Florida. Here, the state constitution assumes the burden of providing "a uniform education" to all of its citizens. This is understood to mean that the state accepts the responsibility to provide a basic education to all of its citizens. It does not require the state to assume the responsibility for meeting every potential need for every student, or even for educating every student to the limits of his or her ability. The state must do its best, with its limited resources, to provide a "uniform" education to all students, assisting those who need help to reach the minimum level of uniform standards. Asking the schools to organize and operate so as to provide enrichment or acceleration beyond a curriculum which provides a uniform education may be unconstitutional.

In fact, the Office of Civil Rights of the United States Department of Education argues that an appropriate, and legal, program for the education of the gifted is required to satisfy two important criteria (Shannon, 1994). First, such programs must be of a type that would provide little opportunity for success to students who are not identified as gifted. Second, such programs must not focus on enrichment activities from which all students in the school would clearly benefit. Programs offered only to gifted students, but in which regular students would be successful and from which they might derive important learnings, are clearly proscribed. How many active programs for gifted students could withstand the scrutiny of a visit from the OCR with these criteria in mind? In fact, the literature on gifted education is virtually bereft of descriptions of actual gifted programs that function effectively and legally (Hunsaker & Callahan, 1993).

Considering the demographic changes currently taking place in American education, the amount of time and effort devoted to meeting the needs of so-called gifted and talented students may be out of all proportion to their representation in the school population. By various definitions these students may represent 1%, 3%, or at most 10% of the students in an average district. By and large, these students are majority culture and middle or upper middle class; frequently they are the sons and daughters of the community's most privileged citizens. These students have no difficulty mastering the uniform curriculum provided by the meager resources of the state. Under the circumstances, the time has come to focus our attention and energy on the 95% of the students who are, more and more, characterized as minorities, the poor, and the unsuccessful. Or, at the very least, advocates for gifted education should be visibly concerned about the lack of diversity in classes and programs for gifted students.

We face a different nation today. It is a nation where every day 40 teenage girls give birth to their third child; where the number of latchkey children has shown a major increase and will continue to do so; where 27% of children live in poverty; where the number of dropouts from our secondary schools is sometimes as high as one out of three, yet 90% of new jobs will require a high school diploma (Hodgkinson, 1988). It is a nation where our international competitiveness depends upon the quality of the average worker every bit as much as it depends upon leadership and management. Granted, all children deserve a quality education, including gifted and talented students, but where should we devote the greater part of our attention and energy?

Conclusion

There is, of course, much more that can and should be said about these concerns. Certainly, many others (Feldman, 1979; Myers & Ridl, 1981; Remley, 1981; Weiler, 1978) have written similarly about these same issues over quite a period of time prior to the current discussions initiated by the more contemporary work of John Goodlad, Jeannie Oakes, and Robert Slavin. The most recent research (e.g., Armstrong, 1993; Gamoran, Nystrand, Berends, & LePore, 1995; Hoffer, 1992; Lee & Smith, 1993; McCaskill, 1993; McElroy, 1993; Meeks, 1993; Mills, 1992; Pallas, Entwisle, Alexander, and Stluka, 1994; Renninger, 1993; Sapon-Shevin, 1994; Swiatek, & Benbow, 1991; Useem, 1992) is even more supportive of the propositions I have offered. Actually, the findings have been fairly consistent for the last 60 years (Whipple, 1936). Nonetheless, advocates for the gifted, with a few notable exceptions (e.g., Renzulli, 1994), continue to singlemindedly reject virtually every option except the separation of gifted students into ability-grouped classes (Feldhusen, 1994).

In order for public schools to remain viable over the next decade, the struggle to balance the demands for both equity and excellence must be successful. In spite of the claims and counterclaims we hurl about, doing away with tracking and ability grouping in a hasty and ill-conceived fashion, and dismantling gifted programs overnight, would almost certainly lead large numbers of upper middle class, majority culture students to abandon the public school in favor of new and attractive private schools or some similar "choice." The resulting public pauper schools would surely be unattractive and dangerous to our future. On the other hand, to continue to practice rigid ability grouping and some gifted programs, as these programs have frequently been operated, may lead to the expansion of elite, quasi-private but publicly-funded academies for honors, advanced, and gifted students within the public schools. Providing exciting and enriching educational experiences for the few, while simultaneously tolerating a very different experience for the remainder must, surely, be unacceptable and dangerous. If we are to successfully avoid these undesirable outcomes, we must all actively care about all of the students, we must be committed to the proposition that a school can only be a good place for one particular group of students if it is a good place for all of the students, and we must care enough to be honest with each other. ■

References

Allen, S. (1991). Ability-grouping research reviews: What do they say about grouping and the gifted? *Educational Leadership, 48* (6), 60-65.

Archambault, F., Westberg, K., & Brown, S. (1992, March). Regular classroom practices with gifted students: Findings from the classroom practices survey. *Newsletter of the National Research Center for Gifted and Talented, 2.*

Armstrong, A. (1993). The effects of cooperative learning on gifted students in heterogeneous and homogeneous groups. *Dissertation Abstracts: International 57* (7), 2457A.

Berliner, D. C. (1993). Mythology and the American system of education. *Phi Delta Kappan, 74*, 632-640.

Blumenfeld, S. (Ed.). (1991a, February). What's wrong with whole language? *The Blumenfeld Education Letter, 6* (2), 1.

Blumenfeld, S. (Ed.). (1991b, June). What's wrong with whole language? *The Blumenfeld Education Letter, 6* (6), 5.

Bracey, G. (1991). "Why can't they be like we were?" *Phi Delta Kappan, 73*, 104-117.

Bracey, G. (October, 1992). The second Bracey report on the condition of public education. *Phi Delta Kappan, 74*, 104-117.

Bracey, G. (1993a). Americans near the top in reading. *Phi Delta Kappan, 74*, 496-97.

Bracey, G. (1993b). The third Bracey report on the condition of public education. *Phi Delta Kappan, 75*, 104-117.

Bracey, G. (1993c). More looks at SIMS. *Phi Delta Kappan, 75*, 187.

Carson, C. C., Huelskamp, R.M., & Woodall, T.D. (1992, April). Perspectives on Education in America. [*The Sandia Report*]. (Reprinted in *The Journal of Educational Research, 86* (5), 259-310).

Cooper, H. (1979). Pygmalion grows up: A model for teacher expectation communication and performance influence. *Review of Educational Research, 49*, 389-406.

Darling-Hammond, L. (1995). Inequality and access to knowledge. In J. Banks (Ed.), *The handbook of research on multicultural education* (pp. 465-483). New York: Macmillan.

Dewey, J. (1944). *Democracy and education.* New York: Free Press.

Erb, T. O. (1992). Encouraging gifted performance in middle schools. *Midpoints Occasional Papers, 3* (1). Columbus, OH: National Middle School Association.

Feldhusen, J. (1991). Full-time classes for gifted youth. *Gifted Child Today, 14* (5), 10-13.

Feldhusen, J. (1992). Grouping gifted students: Issues and concerns. *Gifted Child Quarterly, 36* (2), 63-67.

Feldhusen, J. (1994). A case for developing America's talent: How we went wrong and where we go now. *Roeper Review, 16,* 231-233.

Feldman, D. (1979). Toward a non-elitist conception of giftedness. *Phi Delta Kappan, 60,* 660-663.

Fiedler-Brand, E., Lange, R., & Winebrenner, S. (1990). *Tracking, ability grouping, and the gifted: Myths and realities.* Glenview, IL: Illinois Association for Gifted Children.

Findley, W., & Bryan, M. (1975). The pros and cons of ability grouping. *Phi Delta Kappa Educational Foundation, Fastback 66,* (12).

Gallagher, J. J. (1988). National agenda for educating gifted students: Statement of priorities. *Exceptional Children, 55,* 107-114.

Gallagher, J. J. (1991). Educational reform, values, and gifted students. *Gifted Child Quarterly, 35* (1), 12-19.

Gamoran, A., Nystrand, M., Berends, M., & LePore, P. (1995). An organizational analysis of the effects of ability grouping. *American Educational Research Journal, 32* (4), 687-715.

Gamoran, A., & Berends, M. (1987). The effects of stratification in secondary schools: Synthesis of survey and ethnographic research. *Review of Educational Research, 57,* 415-435.

George, P. (1989). *The Japanese junior high school: An inside look.* Columbus, OH: National Middle School Association.

George, P. (1995). *The Japanese secondary school: A closer look.* Columbus: National Middle School Association.

Good, T., & Brophy, J. (1987). *Looking in classrooms* (4th ed.). New York: Harper and Row.

Hodgkinson, H. (1988). *Florida: The state and its educational system.* Washington, DC: Institute for Educational Leadership.

Hodgkinson, H. (1993). American education: The good, the bad, and the task. *Phi Delta Kappan, 74,* 619-623.

Hoffer, T.B. (1992). Middle school ability grouping and student achievement in science and mathematics. *Educational Evaluation and Policy Analysis, 14,* 205-227.

Hunsaker, S., & Callahan, C. (1993). Evaluation of gifted programs: Current practices. *Journal for the Education of the Gifted, 16,* 190-200.

Joyce, B. (1991). Common misconceptions about cooperative learning and gifted students. *Educational Leadership, 48* (6), 72-74.

Kozol, J. (1991). *Savage inequalities.* New York: Crown.

Kulik, J. (l992). *An analysis of the research on ability grouping: Historical and contemporary perspectives.* Storrs, CT: The National Research Center on the Gifted and Talented.

Kulik, J., & Kulik, C-L. (1984). Effects of ability grouping on secondary school students: A meta-analysis of evaluation findings. *American Educational Research Journal, 19,* 415-428.

Kulik, J., & Kulik, C-L. (1991). Ability grouping and gifted students. In N. Colangelo & G. Davis. (Eds.), *Handbook of Gifted Education* (pp. 178-196). Boston: Simon and Schuster.

Lederer, G. (June, 1992). The calligraphy on the wall? *Education Week, 11* (39), 34.

Lee, V., & Smith, J. (1993). Effects of school restructuring on the achievement and engagement of middle grade students. *Sociology of Education, 66,* 164-187

Males, M. (1992). Top school problems are myths. *Phi Delta Kappan, 74,* 54-56.

McCaskill, L. (1993). Tracking and credit counting in mathematics: A case study at a NYC high school. *Dissertation Abstracts International, 54* (3), 852A.

McElroy, K. (1993). Two worlds of science: An examination of an enriched and a general science class. *Dissertation Abstracts International, 54* (5), 1658A.

Meeks, W. A. (1993). The effects of classroom ability grouping on eighth grade student achievement in mathematics. *Dissertation Abstracts International, 54,* 2933A.

Mills, J. (1992). The effects of grouping in rural elementary schools. *Dissertation Abstracts International, 54* (4), 1181A.

Myers, D., & Ridl, J. (1981). Aren't all children gifted? *Today's Education*, 30GS-33GS.

Noland, T., & Taylor, B. (1986, April). *The effects of ability grouping: A meta-analysis of research*. Paper presented at the meeting of the American Educational Research Association, San Francisco.

Oakes, J. (1985). *Keeping track: How schools structure inequality*. New Haven, CT: Yale University Press.

Oakes, J. (1988). Tracking: Can schools take a different route? *NEA Today, 6* (6), 41-47.

Oakes, J. (1990, July). *Multiplying inequalities: The effects of race, social class, and tracking on opportunities to learn mathematics and science*. Santa Monica, CA: The Rand Corporation.

Page, R. (1991). *Lower-track classrooms: A curricular and cultural perspective*. New York: Teachers College Press.

Pallas, A., Entwisle, D., Alexander, K., & Stluka, M. (1994). Ability group effects: instructional, social, or institutional? *Sociology of Education, 67*, 27-46.

Power, A. M. R. (1994, April). *The effects of tracking on high school students' self esteem*. Paper presented at the meeting of the American Educational Research Association, New Orleans, LA.

Reis, S., & Purcell, J. (1993). An analysis of content elimination and strategies used by elementary classroom teachers in the curriculum compacting process. *Journal of the Education of the Gifted, 16*, 147-170.

Reis, S. (1994, April). *Do advocates for the gifted and detracking folks have anything in common?* Remarks during a panel at the meeting of the American Educational Research Association, New Orleans, LA.

Remley, A. (1981, May). All the best for the brightest—but what about the other 95 percent? *The Progressive, 45*, 44-47.

Renninger, A. (1993). First steps toward reduced tracking. New York University. Dissertation Abstracts International, 54 (7), 2417A.

Renzulli, J. (1994). *Schools for talent development*. Mansfield Center, CT: Creative Learning Press, Inc.

Robinson, A. (1990). Cooperation or exploitation? The argument against cooperative learning for talented students. *Journal for the Education of the Gifted, 14*, 9-27.

Rogers, K. (1991). *The relationship of grouping practices to the education of the gifted and talented learner.* Storrs, CT: The National Research Center on the Gifted and Talented.

Rosenbaum, J. (1976). *Making inequality: The hidden curriculum of high school tracking.* New York: Wiley and Sons.

Sapon-Shevin, M. (1994). *Playing favorites: Gifted education and the disruption of community.* Albany, NY: State University of New York Press.

Shannon, B. (1994, July). *Ability grouping and the office of civil rights.* Presentation made at the conference on Alternatives to Ability Grouping, Orlando, FL.

Sicola, P. (1990). Where do gifted students fit? An examination of the middle school philosophy as it relates to ability grouping and the gifted learner. *Journal for the Education of the Gifted, 14,* 37-49.

Singal, D.J. (1991, November). The other crisis in American education. *Atlantic Monthly, 268* (5), 59-74.

Snider, T. (1989). *Digest of education statistics: 1989.* Washington, DC: U.S. Government Printing Office.

Slavin, R. (1987). Ability grouping and achievement in elementary schools: A best evidence synthesis. *Review of Educational Research, 57,* 293-336.

Slavin, R. (1990a). Achievement effects of ability grouping in secondary schools: A best-evidence synthesis. *Review of Educational Research, 60,* 471-499.

Slavin, R. (1990b). Ability grouping, cooperative learning, and the gifted. *Journal for the Education of the Gifted, 14,* 3-8.

Slavin, R. (1991). Are cooperative learning and 'untracking' harmful to the gifted? *Educational Leadership, 48* (6), 68-71.

Slavin, R. (1993). Ability grouping in the middle grades: Achievement effects and alternatives. *Elementary School Journal, 93,* 535-552.

Stevenson, H., & Lee, S. (1990). Contexts of achievement: A study of American, Chinese, and Japanese children. *Monographs of the Society for Research in Child Development, 55* (1-2, Serial No. 221).

Swiatek, M., & Benbow, C. (1991). Ten-year longitudinal follow-up of ability-matched accelerated and unaccelerated gifted students. *Journal of Educational Psychology, 83,* 528-538.

Useem, E. (1992). Middle schools and math groups: Parents' involvement in children's placement. *Sociology of Education, 65,* 263-279.

Weiler, D. (1978). The alpha children: California's brave new world for the gifted. *Phi Delta Kappan, 60* (3), 185-189.

Whipple, G. M. (Ed.). (1936). *The 35th annual yearbook of the National Society for the Study of Education: Part One. The grouping of pupils.* Bloomington, IL: The Public School Publishing Company.

III

Giftedness in Middle School Students: A Talent Development Perspective

Joseph S. Renzulli
Sally M. Reis

Equity is not the product of similarity;
it is the cheerful acknowledgment of difference.
— Harlan Cleveland, President
World Academy of Art and Science

O f all the innovations, movements, __isms, and ideologies that have paraded through the hallowed halls of education, the one that shows the greatest potential for real and lasting change is middle school education. Most educational reform movements lay battered and broken on the roadside of school improvement because their proponents knew more about what they were against than what they stood for. Progressive education, open education, the behavioral objectives movement, individually guided education, management by objectives, the accountability movement, and a host of other flavor-of-the-month "innovations" are only a few examples of bold, but relatively short-lived, efforts to bring about large-scale improvements in our nation's schools. The middle school movement, however, has built its agenda on a solid foundation of beliefs and resolutions forcefully and unequivocally set forth in position statements such as *This We Believe* (National Middle School Association, 1992, 1995) and *Turning Points* (Carnegie Council on Adolescent Development, 1989).

Middle level education, however, is not without its critics, and the one criticism that stands out above all others is that the middle school movement has devalued rigorous academic and intellectual development in favor of social and emotional development. These critics often point to studies of international comparisons. For example, the U.S. Department of Education (1993) reported that in an international study of 20 countries assessing 9- and 13-year-olds in mathematics and science, the top 10% of American students ranked close to the bottom when compared to the top 10% of the other countries in all areas except science for the 9-year-olds. Related issues such as ability grouping, cooperative learning, curricular differentiation, the development of self-esteem, and concerns about continuing special services for high-achieving students that were initiated in elementary schools have all become sub-issues in the controversy between academic rigor and the attention paid to social and emotional concerns of middle school students. Because the middle school is a crucial link in the pipeline that leads to advanced courses in high school and the transition to competitive colleges and universities, many parents of high-achieving students have expressed concerns about a lack of rigor in the middle school curriculum.

Many middle school educators have responded to the controversy by examining options that attempt to strike a balance between total heterogeneity of experience on one hand and a broad range of differentiated learning opportunities on the other. Remarkably, these responses have caused controversies *within* the middle school movement, mainly between school-level practitioners who are attempting to respond to parental concerns, and some leaders of the movement who believe any deviation from a total philosophy of heterogeneity is equivalent to an act of disloyalty! A strong word, indeed, but this has become a passionate controversy. This passion came to our attention in a forceful way when we presented alternatives for middle level differentiation at a state conference attended by a large number of middle level educators. A middle school principal and a small group of teachers asked to meet "in private." After expressing concern about the need for a meeting site where others could not observe us, they described what some might consider to be intimidation directed at their desire to raise questions about what they called "the party line." The principal said that a popular "game" being played relates to lists of "outstanding middle schools" that circulate around their state, and that virtually the only criterion for being on or off the list is the school's position on the grouping issue. One teacher said pressure to conform to a philosophy of total heterogeneity was unusually strong among some of her team members because of influence exerted from an outside consultant who evaluated their program, and another teacher commented that the teaming process has broken down because of divided opinions about grouping and differentiation.

Progress and Change

It is for these reasons that a crucial issue must be considered *before* we examine the need for grouping alternatives and other forms of differentiation. Simply stated, this issue is whether or not middle level educators are willing to examine possible variations and interpretations in practice and whether individuality can be a part of the "middle school philosophy." Is there room for compromise on the grouping issue? Can we introduce differentiated practices that honor and respect individual diversity in the same way we expect respect for the uniqueness of the middle school as a whole? And can a rigorous and demanding curriculum coexist peacefully with legitimate concerns for the social and emotional development of middle school students? Is the middle school philosophy indelibly etched in stone, or are there conditions in which variations are honored rather than just tolerated? George Bernard Shaw once said, "Progress is impossible without change, and those who cannot change their minds cannot change anything." We believe that reaching the twofold goals of enjoyment and challenge should be the overriding mission of education at all levels, and we further believe that enjoyment and challenge can be produced in all students if we develop specific and practical means for capitalizing on the interdependence of these two goals.

It is also for these reasons that our work, which has its roots in gifted education, has enjoyed growing popularity among middle level educators. The total school enrichment model described in this chapter is regarded by some middle school persons as a compromise between the current middle school philosophy and a focus on the academic and intellectual needs of high achieving students. Both sets of needs are equally important, and the continued success of the middle school movement will undoubtedly depend on a willingness to acknowledge the equal importance of both cognitive and affective needs and to develop ways that both can be met in our classrooms. Buescher (1985) described adolescence as a lengthy period of development in which a young person learns how to be different from others and how to fully belong. He described the following additional challenges that face gifted adolescents: accepting ownership of their abilities, rectifying expected levels of achievement with actual levels of achievement, balancing the need to be in control with the opportunity for personal growth that occurs when academic and personal risks are taken, responding to the expectations of others, dealing with a low tolerance for unresolved situations, and forming an adult-like identity too early that eliminates the exploration of future careers.

The middle school movement started as a plan to reform the junior high school in which, historically, the 7th and 8th grades resembled the elementary school while the 9th grade resembled the high school (Grantes, Noyce, Patterson, & Robertson, 1961). From 1970 to 1990, the number of schools identified as junior high schools declined by 50 percent, while the number of schools that referred to themselves as middle schools increased by over 200 percent (George, Stevenson, Thomason, & Beane, 1992). Many districts may have created middle schools in response to desegregation, changing demographics, and state mandates (George et al., 1992), and by the late 1980s, many districts implemented middle schools according to a philosophy that stressed responsiveness to the characteristics and needs of young adolescent learners (George & Oldaker, 1985a, 1985b). The philosophy of the middle school has been articulated in four national studies (Alexander

& McEwin, 1989; Cawelti, 1988; Carnegie Council on Adolescent Development, 1989; Epstein, 1990). This philosophy stresses a strong emphasis on the affective life of the student; interdisciplinary content; a curriculum emphasizing inquiry, exploration, and discovery; team teaching; and flexible scheduling. These aspects of the middle school philosophy are compatible with education for high ability students (Coleman & Gallagher, 1992; Shore, Cornell, Robinson, & Ward, 1991).

Many high ability youth do poorly in school during adolescence. Recently, Seeley (1988) reviewed the academic records of 2,000 middle school students scoring in the top 25% on standardized tests. He found that 37% were performing academically in the average to failing range. In a review of the academic records of 65 high school students identified as intellectually gifted on the basis of test scores, Fehrenbach (1993) found that 10% of the students failed two or more subjects. Janos and Robinson's (1985) research indicated that some gifted students who had achieved in elementary school rejected labels of excellence in adolescence. Bruns (1992) described a dramatic increase in seventh grade in the percent of students who fail to complete or pass in school work, with 24% of the students in one school system falling into this pattern, most of whom scored in the above average to superior intellectual range on IQ tests. Toepfer (1980) called this the "turn-off syndrome" because students who had achieved As and Bs in elementary school began to receive failing grades in junior high and continued to receive failing grades in high school.

Middle schools that are structured with interdisciplinary teams can develop the capacity to accommodate students with different learning needs – from remediation to acceleration and enrichment. Learning specialists (e.g., teachers of the gifted) who are members of a core interdisciplinary team interact with subject specialists (e.g., English teachers) to offer advice on how to meet the special needs of identified students. Consequently, Erb (1992) believes that "it would appear that the interdisciplinary team practicing collaborative consultation is an ideal arrangement for meeting the needs of gifted learners as well as learners with every other kind of uniqueness" (p. 19), and has offered numerous suggestions for how this can be accomplished (Erb & Doda, 1989).

The purpose of this chapter, therefore, is to present a point of view and a model for school improvement that attempts to achieve a *rapprochement* between what in some cases has degenerated into a mudslinging situation between persons who hold opposing positions about the right and proper educational focus of the middle school. As is always the case in mudslinging contests, each side quickly becomes adept at targeting worst-case examples of the opposition's practices, blaming one another for any perceived differences between the ideal and the reality of recommended practices, and selectively invoking "the research" to defend or attack differing points of view. Yes, there are parents of high achieving students who have been exuberant in their pressure to have the schools better serve their children, but before we criticize them we must remember that most educators consistently try to solicit more parent involvement in their children's education. And yes, there is research that points out some of the negative effects of grouping, but there is also research that supports the benefits of various kinds of grouping. In this chapter, we will explore a middle ground to middle level education and a recommended approach that strikes a balance between opposing positions on grouping and differentiation. An attempt will also be made to show the value of special programs as vehicles that hold promise for improving general practice.

This chapter is divided into four sections. The first section deals with a conception of giftedness that differs from the traditional manner in which most educators and lay persons have viewed this concept. This is an important starting point for our discussion because many middle level educators, and others as well, tend to focus their criticism of special services for the gifted on an older and more conservative point of view. The second section focuses on a major concern about the level of challenge in the curriculum, and why curriculum modification techniques for individual students must be the "bedrock" of any school program that respects differences in learners. The third section dis-

cusses, head on, major dimensions of the grouping issue and offers a
rationale for various kinds of grouping within the middle school. The
fourth section presents a bird's eye view of the Schoolwide Enrichment
Model (SEM), which is a comprehensive plan for achieving both
excellence and equity in the complex challenge to make schools more
effective and enjoyable places for all students. The final section describes some exemplary middle school programs that have implemented
the Schoolwide Enrichment Model and how programs for high achieving students can serve as laboratories for finding new ways to infuse
challenging learning and teaching practices into the process of total
school improvement.

A Broadened Conception of Giftedness

The field of gifted education, like any other specialized area of study,
represents a spectrum of ideologies that exists along a continuum
ranging from conservative to liberal points of view. Conservative and
liberal are not used here in their political connotations, but rather
according to the degree of restrictiveness that is used in determining
who is eligible for special programs and services.

Restrictiveness can be expressed in two ways. First, a definition
can limit the number of specific performance areas that are considered
in determining eligibility for special services. A conservative definition,
for example, might limit eligibility to academic performance only and
exclude other areas such as music, art, drama, leadership, public
speaking, social service, creative writing, or skills in interpersonal
relations. Second, a definition can limit the degree or level of excellence
that one must attain by establishing extremely high cutoff points.

At the conservative end of the continuum is Terman's (1926)
definition of giftedness as "the top one percent level in general intellectual ability as measured by the Stanford-Binet Intelligence Scale or a
comparable instrument" (1926, p. 43). In this definition, restrictiveness
is present in terms of both the type of performance specified (i.e., how

well one scores on an intelligence test) and the level of performance one must attain to be considered gifted (top 1%). At the other end of the continuum can be found more liberal definitions, such as the following one by Witty (1958):

> There are children whose outstanding potentialities in art, in writing, or in social leadership can be recognized largely by their performance. Hence, we have recommended that the definition of giftedness be expanded and that we consider any child gifted whose performance, in a potentially valuable line of human activity, is consistently remarkable. (p. 62)

Although liberal definitions have the obvious advantage of expanding the conception of giftedness, they also open up two "cans of worms" by introducing a values issue (What are the potentially valuable lines of human activity?) and the age-old problem of subjectivity in measurement.

In recent years the values issue has been largely resolved. Very few educators cling tenaciously to a "straight IQ" or purely academic definition of giftedness. "Multiple talent," "talent development," and "multiple criteria" are almost the bywords of the present-day gifted student movement, and most persons would have little difficulty in accepting a definition that includes almost every area of human activity that manifests itself in a socially useful form of expression.

The problem of subjectivity in measurement is not as easily resolved. As the definition of giftedness is extended beyond those abilities that are clearly reflected in tests of intelligence, achievement, and academic aptitude, it becomes necessary to put less emphasis on precise estimates of performance and potential and more emphasis on the opinions of qualified human judges in making decisions about admission to special programs. The crux of the issue boils down to a simple and yet very important question: How much of a trade-off are we willing to make on the objective-subjective continuum in order to allow recognition of a broader spectrum of human abilities? If some degree of subjectivity cannot be tolerated, then our definition of giftedness and the resulting programs will logically be limited to abilities that can be measured only by objective tests.

Two kinds of giftedness

A second issue that must be addressed is that our present efforts to define giftedness are based on a long history of previous studies dealing with human abilities. Most of these studies focused mainly on the concept of intelligence and are briefly discussed here to establish an important point about the process of defining concepts rather than any attempt to equate intelligence with giftedness. Although a detailed review of these studies is beyond the scope of the present chapter, a few of the general conclusions from earlier research (Neisser, 1979) are necessary to set the stage for this analysis.

The first conclusion is that intelligence is not a unitary concept, but rather there are many kinds of intelligence, and, therefore, single definitions cannot be used to explain this multifaceted phenomenon. The confusion and inconclusiveness about present theories of intelligence has led Sternberg (1984) and others to develop new models for explaining this complicated concept. Sternberg's "triarchic" theory of human intelligence consists of three subtheories: a contextual subtheory, which relates intelligence to the external world of the individual; a two-facet experiential subtheory, which relates intelligence to both the external and internal worlds of the individual; and a componential subtheory, which relates intelligence to the internal world of the individual. The contextual subtheory defines intelligent behavior in terms of purposive adaptation to, selection of, and shaping of real-world environments relevant to one's life. The experiential subtheory further constrains this definition by regarding as most relevant to the demonstration of intelligence contextually intelligent behavior that involves either adaptation to novelty or automatization of information processing, or both. The componential subtheory specifies the mental mechanisms responsible for the learning, planning, execution, and evaluation of intelligent behavior.

In view of this recent work and numerous earlier cautions about the dangers of trying to describe intelligence through the use of single scores, it seems safe to conclude that this practice has been and always will be questionable. At the very least, attributes of intelligent behavior must be considered within the context of cultural and situational factors. Indeed, some of the most recent examinations have concluded that "[t]he concept of intelligence cannot be explicitly defined, not only because of the nature of intelligence but also because of the nature of concepts" (Neisser, 1979, p. 179).

A second conclusion is that there is no ideal way to measure intelligence, and therefore we must avoid the typical practice of believing that if we know a person's IQ score, we also know his or her intelligence. Even Terman warned against total reliance on tests: "We must guard against defining intelligence solely in terms of ability to pass the tests of a given intelligence scale" (Thorndike, 1921, p. 131). Thorndike echoed Terman's concern by stating "to assume that we have measured some general power which resides in [the person being tested] and determines his ability in every variety of intellectual task in its entirety is to fly directly in the face of all that is known about the organization of the intellect" (Thorndike, 1921, p. 126).

The reason we have cited these concerns about the historical difficulty of defining and measuring intelligence is to highlight the even larger problem of isolating a unitary definition of giftedness. At the very least, we will always have several conceptions (and therefore definitions) of giftedness. To help in this analysis, we will begin by examining two broad categories of giftedness that have been dealt with in the research literature: "schoolhouse giftedness" and "creative-productive giftedness." Before describing each type, we want to emphasize that:

1. Both types are important.
2. There is usually an interaction between the two types.
3. Special programs should make appropriate provisions for encouraging both types of giftedness as well as the numerous occasions when the two types interact with each other.

Schoolhouse Giftedness. Schoolhouse giftedness might also be called test-taking or lesson-learning giftedness. It is the kind most easily measured by IQ or other cognitive ability tests, and for this reason it is also the type most often used for selecting students for entrance into special programs. The abilities people display on IQ and aptitude tests are exactly the kinds of abilities most valued in traditional school learning situations. In other words, the games people play on ability tests are similar in nature to games that teachers require in most lesson-learning situations. A large body of research tells us that students who score high on IQ tests are also likely to get high grades in school, and that these test-taking and lesson-learning abilities generally remain stable over time (Cronbach & Snow, 1977; Jones & Bayley, 1941; Moffitt, Caspi, Harkness, & Silva, 1993). The results of this research should lead us to some very obvious conclusions about schoolhouse giftedness: It exists in varying degrees; it can be identified through standardized assessment techniques; and we should, therefore, do everything in our power to make appropriate modifications for students who have the ability to cover regular curricular material at advanced rates and levels of understanding. Curriculum compacting (Renzulli, Smith, & Reis, 1982; Reis, Burns, & Renzulli, 1992), a procedure used for modifying curricular content to accommodate advanced learners, and other acceleration techniques should represent an essential part of every school program that strives to respect the individual differences that are clearly evident from scores yielded by cognitive ability tests.

Creative-Productive Giftedness. If scores on IQ tests and other measures of cognitive ability only account for a limited proportion of the common variance with school grades, we can be equally certain that these measures do not tell the whole story when it comes to making predictions about creative-productive giftedness. Before defending this assertion with some research findings, let us briefly review what is meant by this second type of giftedness, the important role that it should play in programming, and, therefore, the reasons we should attempt to assess it in our identification procedures – even if such assessment causes us to look below the top 3-5% on the normal curve of IQ scores.

Creative-productive giftedness describes those aspects of human activity and involvement where a premium is placed on the development of original material and products that are purposefully designed to have an impact on one or more target audiences. Learning situations that are designed to promote creative-productive giftedness emphasize the use and application of information (content) and thinking skills in an integrated, inductive, and real-problem-oriented manner. The role of the student is transformed from that of a learner of prescribed lessons to one in which she or he uses the *modus operandi* of a firsthand inquirer. This approach is quite different from the development of lesson-learning giftedness that tends to emphasize deductive learning, structured training in the development of thinking processes, and the acquisition, storage, and retrieval of information. In other words, creative-productive giftedness is simply putting one's abilities to work on problems and areas of study that have personal relevance to the student and that can be escalated to appropriately challenging levels of investigative activity. The roles that both students and teachers should play in the pursuit of these problems have been described elsewhere (Renzulli, 1977, 1982) and have been embraced in general education under the concepts of authentic learning and performance assessment.

Why is creative-productive giftedness important enough for us to question the "tidy" and relatively easy approach that traditionally has been used to select students on the basis of test scores? Why do some people want to rock the boat by challenging a conception of giftedness that can be numerically defined by simply giving a test? The answers to these questions are simple and yet very compelling. A review of the research literature (Renzulli, 1986) tells us that there is much more to identifying human potential than the abilities revealed on traditional tests of intelligence, aptitude, and achievement. Furthermore, history tells us it has been the creative and productive people of the world, the producers rather than consumers of knowledge, the reconstructionists of thought in all areas of human endeavor, who have become recognized as "truly gifted" individuals. History does not remember persons who merely scored well on IQ tests or those who learned their lessons well.

A change in direction: From being gifted to the development of gifted behaviors and schools for talent development

Up to this time, the general approach to the study of gifted persons could easily lead the casual reader to believe that giftedness is an absolute condition that is magically bestowed upon a person in much the same way that nature endows us with blue eyes, red hair, or a dark complexion. This position is not supported by the research. For too many years we have pretended that we can identify gifted children in an absolute and unequivocal fashion. Many people have come to believe that certain individuals have been endowed with a golden chromosome that makes him or her "a gifted person." This belief has further led to the mistaken idea that all we need to do is find the right combination of factors that prove the existence of this "gift." The use of terms such as "the truly gifted," "the highly gifted," the "moderately gifted," and the "borderline gifted" only serve to confound the issue because they invariably harken back to a conception of giftedness that equates the concept with test scores. The misuse of the concept of giftedness has given rise to a great deal of criticism and confusion about both identification and programming. The result has been that so many mixed messages have been sent to educators and the public that both groups now have a justifiable skepticism about the credibility of the gifted education establishment and our ability to offer services that are qualitatively different from general education.

Most of the confusion and controversy surrounding the definitions of giftedness that have been offered by various writers can be placed into proper perspective if we examine a few key questions. Is giftedness an absolute or relative concept? That is, is a person either gifted or not gifted (the absolute view), or can varying degrees of gifted behaviors be developed in certain people, at certain times, and under certain circumstances (the relative view)? Is giftedness a static concept (i.e., you have or you do not have it), or is it a dynamic concept (i.e., it varies within persons and among learning/performance situations)?

These questions have led us to advocate a fundamental change in the ways the concept of giftedness should be viewed in the future. Except for certain functional purposes related mainly to professional focal points (i.e., research, training, legislation) and to ease-of-expression, we believe that labeling students as "the gifted" is counterproductive to the educational efforts aimed at providing supplementary educational experiences for certain students in the general school population. For over 15 years, we have advocated *labeling the services students receive rather than labeling the students*. We believe that our field should shift its emphasis from a traditional concept of "being gifted" (or not being gifted) to a concern about the *development of gifted behaviors* in students who have high potential for benefiting from special educational services. This slight shift in terminology might appear to be an exercise in heuristic hair splitting, but it has significant implications for the entire way that we think about the concept of giftedness and the ways in which we should nurture the development of gifted behaviors in young people. This change in terminology may also provide the flexibility in both identification and programming endeavors that will encourage the inclusion of at-risk and underachieving students in our programs. If that occurs, not only will we be giving these high potential youngsters an opportunity to participate, we will also help to eliminate the charges of elitism and bias in grouping that are sometimes legitimately directed at particular programs. Our ultimate goal is the development of a total school enrichment program that benefits all students and concentrates on making schools places for talent development in young people.

Kelvin. Two afternoons a week, 12-year-old Kelvin goes to an enrichment cluster at the Quirk Middle School in an urban area in Connecticut. When he was selected for the program, Kelvin said, "It feels good, but I was amazed. I was about to faint! I was super, super surprised." The reason for Kelvin's amazement is that he never considered himself to be a good student, at least not in the traditional way we usually view students. And the program was not exactly the place where you found kids like Kelvin, who lives in subsidized housing and whose family manages to survive on a monthly welfare check and food stamps.

But the program Kelvin is enrolled in looks at talent development in a different way. Based on a plan called the Schoolwide Enrichment Model, the program seeks to identify a broad range of talent potentials in all students through the use of a strength assessment guide called the Total Talent Portfolio. This guide helps to focus attention on student interests and learning style preferences as well as strengths in traditional subjects. These strengths serve as building blocks for advanced achievement. Kelvin's strongest academic area is mathematics, and through a process called curriculum compacting, he is now being provided with mathematics material that is two grade levels above the level of math being covered in his classroom.

Kelvin, who once described himself as a "mental dropout," now finds school a much more inviting place. He is hoping to enter the research he is doing on airplane wing design in his enrichment cluster into the state science fair competition. He is also thinking about a career in engineering, and the enrichment specialist at his school has helped him apply for a special summer program at the University of Connecticut that is designed to recruit and assist minorities interested in mathematical and engineering related professions. "School," says Kelvin, "is a place where you have must-dos and can-dos. I work harder on my must-dos so I can spend more time working on my can-dos."

Kelvin represents one example of the ways in which numerous students are being given opportunities to develop talent potentials that too many schools have ignored for too many years. The type of program in which Kelvin is enrolled is not a radical departure from present school structures, but it is based on assumptions about learners and learning that are different from those that have guided public education for many years. The factory model of schooling that gave rise to the clear and present danger facing our schools cannot be used to overcome the very problems that this model of schooling has created. As Albert

Einstein said, "Problems can not be solved at the same level of consciousness that created them." And yet, as we examine reform initiatives, it is difficult to find plans and policies that are qualitatively different from the old top-down patterns of school organization or the traditional linear/sequential models of learning that have dominated almost all of the curriculum used in our schools. Transcending these previous levels of consciousness will not be an easy task. If there is any single, unifying characteristic of present day schools, that characteristic is surely a resistance, if not an immunity, to change. The ponderous rhetoric about school improvement and the endless lists of noble goals need to be tempered with a gentle and evolutionary approach to change that school personnel can live with and grow with rather than be threatened by. If the traditional methods of schooling have failed to bring about substantial changes, we must look at different models that have shown promise for achieving the types of school improvement we have so desperately sought.

One such model has been developed during the last twenty years of research and field testing at The University of Connecticut (Renzulli & Reis, 1994). The Schoolwide Enrichment Model (SEM) is a systematic set of specific strategies for increasing student effort, enjoyment, and performance, and for integrating a broad range of enrichment and accelerated learning experiences into any curricular area, course of study, or pattern of school organization. The general approach of the SEM is one of infusing more effective practices into existing school structures rather than layering on additional things for schools to do. This research supported plan, which will be described in a later section of this chapter, is designed for general education, but is based on a large number of instructional methods and curricular practices that had their origins in special programs for high ability students.

The Secret Laboratories of School Improvement. In many respects, special programs of almost any type have been the true laboratories of our nation's schools because they have presented ideal opportunities for testing new ideas and experimenting with potential solutions to long-standing educational problems. Programs for high potential students have been an especially fertile place for experimentation because such programs usually are not encumbered by prescribed curriculum guides or traditional methods of instruction. It was within the context of these programs that the thinking skills movement first took hold in American education, and the pioneering work of notable theorists such as Benjamin Bloom, Howard Gardner, and Robert Sternberg first gained the attention of the education community. Other developments that had their origins in special programs are currently being examined for general practice and have been embraced by many educators within the middle school movement. These developments include a focus on concept rather than skill learning; the use of interdisciplinary curriculum and theme-based studies; student portfolios; performance assessment; cross-grade grouping; alternative scheduling patterns; and perhaps most important, opportunities for students to exchange traditional roles as lesson-learners and doers-of-exercises for more challenging and demanding roles that require hands-on learning, firsthand investigations, and the application of knowledge and thinking skills to complex problems.

Research opportunities in a variety of special programs have enabled us to develop instructional procedures and programming alternatives that emphasize the need to provide a broad range of advanced level enrichment experiences for all students and to use the many and varied ways that students respond to these experiences as stepping stones for relevant follow-up on the parts of individuals or small groups. This approach is not viewed as a new way to identify who is or is not "gifted"! Rather, the process simply identifies how subsequent *opportunities, resources,* and *encouragement* can be provided to support continuous escalations of student involvement in both required and self-selected activities. This approach to the development of high levels of multiple potentials in young people is purposefully designed to sidestep the traditional practice of labeling some students "gifted" (and by implication, relegating all others to the category of "not-gifted"). The term "gifted" is used in our lexicon only as an adjective, and even then, it is used in a developmental perspective. Thus, for example, we speak and write about *the development of gifted behaviors* in specific areas of learning and human expression rather than giftedness as a state of being. This orientation has allowed many students opportunities to develop high levels of creative and productive accomplishments that otherwise would have been denied through traditional special program models.

Practices that have been a mainstay of many special programs for "the gifted" are being absorbed into general education by reform models designed to upgrade the performance of all students. This integration of gifted program know-how is viewed as a favorable development for two reasons. First, the adoption of many special program practices is indicative of the viability and usefulness of both the know-how of special programs and the role enrichment specialists can and should play in total school improvement. It is no secret that compensatory education in the U.S. has largely been a failure! An overemphasis on remedial and mastery models has lowered the challenge level of the very population that programs such as Chapter I attempts to serve. Second, all students should have opportunities to develop higher order thinking skills and to pursue more rigorous content and firsthand investigative activities than those typically found in today's "dumbed down" text-books. The ways in which students respond to enriched learning experiences should be used as a rationale for providing all students with advanced level follow-up opportunities. This approach reflects a democratic ideal that accommodates the full range of individual differences in the entire student population, and it opens the door to programming models that develop potential talents of many at-risk students who traditionally have been excluded from anything but the most basic types of curricular experiences. But in order to operationalize this ideal, we need to get serious about the things we have learned during the past several years about both programming models and human potential.

The application of gifted program know-how into general educa-tion is supported by a wide variety of research on human abilities

(Bloom, 1985; Gardner, 1983; Renzulli, 1986; Sternberg, 1984). This research clearly and unequivocally provides a justification for much broader conceptions of talent development. These conceptions argue against the restrictive student selection practices that have guided identification procedures in the past. Lay persons and professionals at all levels have begun to question the efficacy of programs that rely on narrow definitions, IQ scores, and other cognitive ability measures as the primary methods for identifying which students can benefit from differentiated services. Traditional identification procedures have restricted services to small numbers of high scoring students and excluded large numbers of at-risk students whose potentials are manifested in other ways. Special services should be viewed as opportunities to develop "gifted behaviors" rather than merely finding and certifying them. In this regard, we should judiciously avoid saying that a young person is either "gifted" or "not gifted."

Liz. It is difficult to gain support for talent development when we use statements such as "Liz is a gifted sixth grader" as a rationale for providing services. These kinds of statements offend many people and raise the accusations of elitism that have plagued special programs. But note the difference in orientation when we focus on the behavioral characteristics that brought this student to our attention in the first place: "Liz is a sixth grader who reads at the adult level and who has a fascination with biographies about women of accomplishment." And note the logical and justifiable services provided for Liz:

1. Under the guidance of her classroom teacher, Liz is allowed to substitute more challenging books in her interest area for the books used in the regular Language Arts curriculum. The Schoolwide Enrichment teaching specialist helps the classroom teacher locate these books, and they are purchased with funds from the enrichment program budget.

2. Liz is able to leave the school two afternoons a month (usually on early dismissal days) to meet with a mentor who is a local journalist specializing in gender issues. The Schoolwide Enrichment

teaching specialist arranges transportation with the help of the school's parent volunteer group.

3. During time made available through curriculum compacting in her strength areas (i.e., reading, language arts, and spelling), the Schoolwide Enrichment teaching specialist helps Liz prepare a questionnaire and interview schedule to be used with local women scientists and female science faculty members at a nearby university.

Could even the staunchest anti-gifted proponent argue against the logic or the appropriateness of these services? When programs focus on developing the behavioral potential of individuals, or small groups who share a common interest, it is no longer necessary to organize groups merely because they all happen to be "gifted sixth graders."

The Need for Curricular Differentiation

The "dumbing down" of textbooks

One reason that so many students who achieve at high levels are unchallenged or underchallenged in school is that contemporary textbooks have been "dumbed down," by as much as two to three years in grade level from the levels at which they were written in the 1940s and 1950s (Kirst, 1982). Chall and Conrad (1991) documented a trend of decreasing difficulty in the most widely used textbooks over a thirty-year period from 1945-1975. "On the whole, the later the copyright dates of the textbooks for the same grade, the easier they were, as measured by indices of readability level, maturity level, difficulty of questions and extent of illustration" (p. 2). Most recently, Altbach, Kelly, Petrie, and Weis (1991) suggested that textbooks, as evaluated across a spectrum of assessment measures, have declined in rigor. Researchers have discussed the particular problems encountered by high ability students when textbooks are "dumbed down" because of read-ability formulas or the politics of textbook adoption. Bernstein (1985) summarized the particular problem that current textbooks pose for gifted and talented students, "Even if there were good rules of thumb about the touchy subject of textbook adoption, the issue becomes moot when a school district buys only one textbook, usually at 'grade level,' for all students in a subject or grade. Such a purchasing policy pressures adoption committees to buy books that the least-able students can read. As a result, the needs of more advanced students are sacrificed" (p. 465). Chall and Conrad (1991) also cite particular difficulties for the above average student with regard to less-difficult-reading textbooks:

> Another group not adequately served was those who read about two grades or more above the norm. Their reading textbooks, especially, provided little or no challenge, since they were matched to students' grade placement, not their reading levels. Many students were aware of this and said, in their interviews, that they preferred harder books because they learned harder words and ideas from them. Since harder reading textbooks are readily available, one may ask why they were not used with the more able readers, as were the easier reading textbooks for the less able readers. (p. 11)

Repetition in content

Recent findings by Usiskin (1987) and Flanders (1987) indicate that not only have textbooks decreased in difficulty, but that they also incorporate a large percentage of repetition to facilitate learning. Usiskin argues that even average eighth grade students should study algebra since only 25% of the pages in typical seventh and eighth grade mathematics texts contain new content. Flanders corroborated this finding by investigating the mathematics textbook series of three popular publishers. Students in upper elementary grades who used these math textbooks encountered approximately 40-65% new content over the course of the school year, which equates to learning new material only two to three days a week. By eighth grade the amount of new content introduced in math textbooks had dropped to 30%, which translates into encountering new material only $1\frac{1}{2}$ days a week. Flanders suggests that these estimates are conservative because the days that students spend reviewing and testing were not included in this analysis. He concluded: "There should be little wonder why good students get bored. They do the same thing year after year" (p. 22).

Repetition in content is also reflected by the scores students attain on pretests that they take before they begin to use their textbooks. For example, a study conducted by the Educational Products Information Exchange Institute revealed that 60% of fourth graders in certain school districts studied were able to achieve a score of 80% or higher on a test of the content of their math texts before they had opened their books in September. In a recent study dealing with average and above readers, Taylor and Frye (1988) found that 78% to 88% of middle school students who were average and above average readers could pass pretests on comprehension skills before they were covered by the basal reader. The average students were performing at approximately 92% accuracy while the better readers were performing at 93% on comprehension skill pretests. The mismatch between what students are capable of doing, what they already know, and the curricular materials they are expected to study becomes even more disturbing when one considers the heavy reliance on textbooks and their declining challenge level.

The mismatch between student ability and instruction

It is clear that students should be matched with curriculum that is appropriate for their achievement level. That is, for learning to occur, instruction should be above the learner's current level of performance. Chall and Conrad (1991) stress the importance of the match between a learner's abilities and the difficulty of the instructional task, stating that the optimal match should place the instructional task slightly above the learner's current level of functioning. When the match is optimal, learning is enhanced. However, "if the match is not optimal [i.e., the match is below or above the child's level of understanding and knowledge], learning is less efficient and development may be halted" (p.19).

It is clear that the current trend of selecting textbooks which the majority of students can read is a problem for high ability students.

A mismatch seems to exist between the difficulty of textbooks, the repetition of curricular material in these texts, and the needs of high achieving learners. It is reasonable to conclude that many of these students spend much of their time in school practicing skills and learning content they already know. All of these factors may be causing high potential students to learn less and may be encouraging their underachievement.

Three recent studies have analyzed whether the needs of high ability students can be met in regular classroom settings. This research presents a disturbing picture of the degree of differentiation taking place in classrooms. The Classroom Practices Survey (Archambault, Westberg, Brown, Hallmark, Emmons, & Zhang, 1992) was conducted by The National Research Center on the Gifted and Talented (NRC/GT) to determine the extent to which high achieving students receive differentiated education in regular classrooms. Six samples of upper elementary grade teachers in public schools, private schools, and schools with high concentrations of four types of ethnic minorities were randomly selected to participate in this research, and over 51% of this national sample of classroom teachers responded to the survey. The survey revealed that 61% of public school teachers and 54% of private school teachers reported that they had never had any training in teaching gifted students. The major finding of this study was that classroom teachers make only minor modifications in the regular curriculum to meet the needs of gifted students. This result holds for all types of schools sampled, for classrooms in various parts of the country, and for various types of communities.

The Classroom Practices Observational Study (Westberg, Archambault, Dobyns, & Salvin, 1992) extended the results of the classroom practices survey by examining the instructional and curricular practices used with gifted and talented students in regular elementary classrooms throughout the United States. Systematic observations were conducted in 46 third or fourth grade classrooms. The observations were designed to determine if and how classroom teachers meet the needs of gifted and talented students in the regular classroom. Two students, one high ability student and one average ability student, were selected as target students for each observation day. The Classroom Practices Record (CPR) was developed to document the types and frequencies of differentiated instruction that gifted students received through modifications in curricular activities, materials, and teacher-student verbal interactions. Descriptive statistics and chi-square procedures were used to analyze the CPR data. The results indicated little differentiation in the instructional and curricular practices, including grouping arrangements and verbal interactions, for gifted and talented students in the regular classroom. Across five subject areas and 92 observation days, gifted students received instruction in homogeneous groups only 21% of the time, and more alarmingly, the targeted gifted and talented or high ability students experienced no instructional or curricular differentiation in 84% of the instructional activities in which they participated.

A content analysis was also conducted on the 92 daily summaries completed by the trained observers. The dominant theme in this content analysis involved the use of identical practices for all students. Phrases such as "no differentiation" and "no purposeful differentiation" appeared on 51 of the 92 daily summaries. Anecdotal summaries provided poignant glimpses into the daily experiences of high ability students, such as the following: "It should be noted that S#1 (the targeted high ability student) was inattentive during all of her classes. She appeared to be sleepy, never volunteered, and was visibly unenthusiastic about all activities. No attempt was made to direct HOTS (higher order thinking skills) questions to her or to engage her in more challenging work. She never acted out in any way."

The Curriculum Compacting Study (Reis, Westberg, Kulikowich, Caillard, Hébert, Purcell, Rogers, & Plucker, 1993) examined the effects of escalating levels of staff development on the teaching practices of teachers throughout the country as they implemented a plan called curriculum compacting (Renzulli, Smith, & Reis, 1982; Reis, Burns, &

Renzulli, 1992) to modify the curriculum for high ability students. Curriculum compacting involves three steps: first, assessing students' academic strengths; second, eliminating skillwork and content that students have already mastered; and third, replacing the work that has been eliminated with more challenging alternatives, some of which are based on students' interests.

Three treatment groups of second through sixth grade teachers from across the country received increasing levels of staff development as they implemented curriculum compacting. A control group of teachers continued with normal teaching practices. Four hundred and thirty-six teachers participated in this study, as did 783 students. Students in both control and treatment groups took the next chrono-logical grade level Iowa Test of Basic Skills in both October and May. When classroom teachers in the treatment group eliminated between 40% and 50% of the regular curriculum for high ability students, no differences were found between treatment and control groups in reading, math computation, social studies, and spelling. Students in the treatment group whose curriculum was compacted in science and math concepts scored significantly higher than their counterparts in the control group. Accordingly, teachers were able to eliminate as much as 40-50% of material without detrimental effects to achievement scores. And in some content areas, scores were actually higher when this elimination of previous mastered content took place.

Common Sense About Grouping

Grouping is an intensely debated issue that has always been the subject of much controversy in American education, and the pendulum between homogeneous and heterogeneous grouping has continued to swing back and forth since the beginning of public education. The present day debate about grouping also carries with it some added baggage about the inclusion of special education students in regular classrooms, the proper way to provide challenging levels of learning for high achieving students, the adequacy of teacher preparation for dealing with an extremely broad range of learning levels within a single classroom, and the under-representation of minorities in advanced level and honors courses and in special programs for the gifted. This last concern has resulted in battle lines being drawn along class and racial lines, which in many cases pits White, middle-class parents and parents of students who participate in traditional "gifted programs" against the parents of students from disadvantaged backgrounds. Some parents of poor and minority students believe that a second-class education, and even racial segregation, is being perpetuated in the form of classes organized according to achievement levels, and that their sons and daughters are being denied equality of educational opportunity because of homogeneous classes. Some middle-class parents, on the other hand, believe that heterogeneous grouped classes slow the rate of learning, drag down achievement test scores, and place their daughters and sons in classes with unmotivated and frequently disruptive students.

The issue is compounded at the middle level because a general commitment to heterogeneous grouping in the middle school philosophy represents a transition from the within-class achievement grouping frequently practiced at the elementary level, especially in basic skill subjects, and the continued widespread practice of establishing advanced level or honors classes at the high school level. Middle-class parents view the middle school curriculum as the beginning of "the pipeline" leading to advanced courses in high school and admission to competitive colleges. These parents argue that a lack of differentiation in the middle school curriculum causes a watered-down high school curriculum, and they frequently gain support for this conclusion from high school teachers of Advanced Placement and honors courses. Declining SAT scores among students at the top of the scoring continuum are also offered as further evidence of declining rigor in the middle schools (Singal, 1991).

Further down the pipeline, persons in higher education are also expressing concern about pre-college preparation. A recent article (Knowlton, 1995) indicated that fully a third of each year's freshman class at U.S. colleges and universities is in need of remedial work and that 85% of the nation's 3600 college campuses offer remedial courses. While it is true that remedial education is found more frequently in two-year community colleges and open enrollment four-year colleges, even the most prestigious universities offer remedial courses and academic tutoring. Syracuse University, for example, offers a credit-bearing course called College Learning Skills 105 to teach students how to study and take notes, and Princeton University offers tutorial programs for entering freshmen who are described by the university as students "whose high schools have not given them the opportunity to study math and science at a level commensurate with the fast paced curriculum they will find here" (p. 17). In an article dealing with declining SAT scores and other indicators of lower national performance, Singal (1991) reported on college level writing:

> [A]ccording to Richard Marius, the director of the expository writing program at Harvard, "the number of words [students have] available to express their thoughts is very, very limited, and the forms by which they express themselves are also very limited. The average incoming Harvard student has a utilitarian command of the language resulting in sentences that follow a simple subject-predicate, subject-predicate format, with little variation in richness of verbal expression." Harvard, of course, gets the cream of the crop. Those of us who teach at lesser institutions would be happy with utilitarian but serviceable prose from our freshmen. More often we get mangled sentences, essays composed without the slightest sense of paragraphing, and writing that can't sustain a thought for more than half a page. (p. 62)

At the local school level, concerns about grouping are expressed by parents in various ways. In Cheshire, Connecticut, for example, a group of middle school parents petitioned the school board to allow students a choice between Algebra I and an Integrated Math I course that replaced the traditional sequence in mathematics. Several persons, including Yale and University of Connecticut math professors, reviewed the integrated math textbooks; and while they found them well-written, they concluded that texts were far below the level of challenge that should be provided for top math students. "All we want is a choice," said one parent whose eighth grade daughter attends the middle school.

In a recent evaluation study conducted at the local school level (Reis, 1994), parents of middle school students who were formerly involved in enrichment programs were asked to complete a questionnaire about their perceptions of the level of challenge their children had encountered in their heterogeneous academic classes at the middle school level. One hundred per cent of the parents responding to the questionnaire indicated that their children were not challenged in their academic classes. The majority of the parents said "no" unequivocally, but two parents did say that their needs were met in one class but not in most. Many parents wrote fairly long and eloquent responses; some were direct and to the point: "Absolutely not," and "NO NO NO. Thank you for finally asking." The following comments were representative of the responses:

> No, my child seems to have less homework and studying now than he did in fifth grade.

> No, the needs of high ability students are not being met in most classes. In our case, our child often describes his school day as pathetically boring.

> No, it is difficult for higher ability students to be challenged while the teacher has to teach to the lower level students, especially in English, social studies, and science. The reading material, especially, is not at all challenging.

Data were also gathered on teachers' perceptions of their ability to meet the needs of high achieving students in their classes, what they did to modify curriculum in their classes, their perceptions of the need for accelerated classes, and an open-ended question about how the district addresses the needs of high ability students. When asked whether they believed they were currently able to meet the needs of high ability students in their classes, 43% of the teachers indicated yes and 57% said no, they were not able to meet the needs of high ability or hihg-achieving students. The teachers who said they could not address the needs of high ability students indicated three reasons for their inability to accomplish this goal. The most frequently cited reasons were the nature of their heterogeneous classes and the amount of time involved to do the job well, which took time away from what could be done to address the needs of high ability or high-achieving students. They also mentioned their lack of materials and students with behavior problems who took time away from the rest of the class.

When asked what types of services they would need to work with high ability students in their classes, teachers responded with the following, in order of frequency: supplies, time, ideas, an enrichment teacher to help with student projects, staff development, and the return to the use of achievement groups which enabled them to have one class of high achieving students out of the thirteen content area classes offered at each grade level. One teacher's comment summarized the comments made by many: "More challenging curriculum, time to assist and encourage research and greater development." It was clear that the middle school teachers who responded to this questionnaire had mixed opinions about their ability to meet the needs of high ability students in their classes. The majority did not believe they were currently address-ing the needs of this group and many were frustrated at what they did not know or have (materials, challenging curriculum) to be able to help these students.

These concerns, up and down the educational pipeline, have implications for the grouping issue and collectively have resulted in unrelenting pressure on school boards, administrators, and policy makers to provide an educational solution to what is largely a broader range of societal problems. These problems include the concentration of low income housing in restricted geographic areas, unequal employment opportunities, inequitable access to adequate health care, the by-products of teenage pregnancy, single parent families, and the despair that surrounds growing up poor in America. These problems, taken collectively, have created strong ideological differences of opinion about how to deal with inequity in our society, and schools have been caught in the middle of these larger societal and ideological issues.

Honest attempts on the parts of educators to respond to these problems typically have been (a) redistricting and busing programs, (b) the creation of regional or magnet schools that are intended to attract students across class and race lines, (c) the redeployment of school resources, and (d) yet another round of regulations on grouping – most of which are unsatisfactory to persons on both sides of the issue. Only two things are clear about the grouping issue. First, grouping will continue to remain the major controversy in American education as long as differences of opinion exist about the role that schools should play *and* can play (two essentially different concerns) in achieving equity and excellence in education. Second, there are no "silver bullets" that will satisfy persons on opposite ends of the controversy; and therefore, a compromise is necessary in order to avoid outright warfare between persons with differing points of view. Before presenting recommendations that represent such a compromise, some of the issues associated with grouping will be discussed.

Grouping vs. tracking

Any discussion of grouping must begin by making a clear distinction between grouping and tracking. Tracking is the general and usually permanent assignment of students to classes that are taught at a certain level and that are usually taught using a whole-group instructional model. Tracking is most prevalent at the secondary school level, and there are several features about tracking that have made it a detrimental procedure, especially for students who end up in low tracks. Critics of tracking contend that a concentration of low achieving students in one classroom almost always results in a curriculum that emphasizes remediation, isolated and repetitive practice of skills like phonics and computation at the expense of problem solving and comprehension, and low expectations for all students in the group (Oakes, 1985; Slavin, 1987; Slavin, 1990; Slavin, Madden, & Stevens, 1990). Critics also say that students are frequently locked into all low or "general" track classes; and, unlike college or vocational tracks, they have a dead-end orientation rather than an orientation toward post-secondary education or entrance into the skilled labor market. This lack of purposefulness frequently results in low motivation and self-esteem, underachievement, behavior problems, absenteeism, and school dropouts.

Low-track classes are usually taught in such a way that they become ends in themselves, rather than as places where students are being prepared to move into higher track classes. Economically disadvantaged students are disproportionately represented in low-track classes, and this practice further reinforces their sense of failure and feelings about the limited value of a formal education. The position of many middle school experts is that tracking provides few benefits to all groups of learners. George (1988) concluded that at the middle level "it appears that only the top ten percent of the students may learn more when tracking is utilized, and the remaining ninety percent may actually learn less" (p. 27).

Grouping, however, can be a very different and much more flexible practice. Several different forms of grouping exist at the middle school level. First, advanced level classes can be offered within content areas. For example, if several sections of mathematics are taught at any given grade level, one class can be designated an advanced class and students can cover content at an accelerated pace within this class. Different students may be able to take advanced classes in different content areas, and students who are found to be working at an advanced level who were not originally scheduled into the advanced classes may be scheduled into these more challenging classes at various times throughout the year. Interest grouping may also be used to enable students to pursue various types of interests in content areas or extracurricular activities. Girls can be clustered in one class who are interested and talented in mathematics or science in an effort to maintain these talents at a time when many other girls become less interested in these subjects. Cluster grouping may also be used to assign students who are achieving at high levels to teachers who will make various types of accommodations within their heterogeneous classrooms. The purpose of cluster grouping is to put students who need these accommodations together so that individual teachers do not have to duplicate efforts and also to enable students who learn at advanced levels to be able to have a group of peers so that they do not feel different or begin to under-achieve because of peer pressures. These are only a few examples of the several types of grouping available at the middle level. Regardless of the types of grouping arrangements used in a school, students should be able to be challenged at appropriately high levels for their achievement.

The politics of "research" about grouping

The argument over grouping has been a long and passionate one, and every faction rattles off its cache of research studies, while simulta-neously pointing out the shortcomings of research presented by the opposition. And like all of the armies that ever took up weapons, each group is convinced that rightness is on *its* side. Adversaries even lay claim to the same study by adding their own surplus interpretation or procedure for reanalyzing the data. The only thing certain about the research on ability grouping and its relation to achievement is that there are well-documented arguments on both sides of the issue (Kulik, 1992; Oakes, 1985; Rogers, 1991; Slavin, 1987, 1990). But let us examine how a few studies which report negative social and attitudinal effects of grouping have been blown out of proportion in the popular press and in non-research journals. In an article in the *Middle School Journal* entitled "Tracking and Grouping: Which Way for the Middle School?" (George, 1988), the author uses the results of a questionnaire to draw conclusions that clearly are not justified by the data. Simply stated, the conclusions were that "good middle schools" were ones that did not group students and that administrators of non-grouped middle schools were considered to be effective and innovative. This study did not gather any achievement data, nor were any data reported about the criteria for evaluating a school or its administrators. The conclusions were reinforced in the article by selected outtakes (large type, bold print quotes) that unanimously favored the anti-grouping position and that were in agreement with an editorial position as set forth in an editor's note preceding the article. A subsequent report sponsored by the National Association of Secondary School Principals (Toepfer, 1990) draws upon this article in a fashion that would lead the casual reader to believe that it is more powerful research than is actually the case; then the report proceeds to highlight yet another string of anti-grouping statements. What has clearly happened is that commentators are using "the research" to support a political issue rather than an educational issue, and "the research" has become little more than a pawn that is being used for political expediency.

The best way to illustrate this accusation about political interpretation of research is to assume for a minute that the research on grouping is inconclusive or neutral and then examine conclusions drawn from grouping studies. Whenever average or below average students fail to show growth in achievement from grouping studies, the almost universal conclusion is that grouping is at fault. But note how a prominent analyst of grouping research distinguishes clearly between the effect of grouping per se and other factors such as curriculum adaptations for students in grouped settings.

> Gifted and special education programs may be conceived of as one form of ability grouping, but they also involve many other changes in curriculum, class size, resources, and goals that make them fundamentally different from comprehensive ability grouping plans....Studies of special programs for the gifted tend to find achievement benefits for the gifted students...[some analysts] would give the impression that ability grouping is beneficial for high achievers and detrimental for low achievers. *However, it is likely that characteristics of special accelerated programs for the gifted account for the effects of gifted programs, not the fact of separate grouping per se.* (Slavin, 1987, p. 307, italics added)

75

Slavin presents a clear message. If positive growth is the result of curriculum adaptations, class size, resources, and goals, why then cannot we apply the same explanation to cases in which growth is not shown? More importantly, can we not use the know-how of educational practices that emerges from studies of favorable achievement to explore ways of promoting better performance in lower achieving students? This is exactly the rationale that underlies the Schoolwide Enrichment Model, which extends the pedagogy of gifted education to all students. But the grouping issue, rather than a focus on what must be done to create favorable acts of learning, has taken center stage, and is offered as a "quick-fix" approach to improving our schools. Gutiérrez and Slavin, pursuing the same distinctions pointed out above, offered an alternative to traditional forms of ability grouping:

> In the nongraded plan, students are flexibly grouped for major subjects (especially reading and math) across class and age lines, so that the resulting groups are truly homo-geneous on the skills being taught. Further, by creating multi-age groups from among all students in contiguous grade levels, it is possible for teachers to create entire reading or math classes at one or, at most, two levels, so that they need not devote much class time to follow-up.
>
> (Gutiérrez & Slavin, 1992, p. 339)

The research summarized by Gutiérrez and Slavin (1992) clearly indicates that multi-age grouping based on the skills being taught has proven to be an effective practice. But we also believe that even within a homogeneous skill level group, provisions must also be made for curriculum compacting and cluster grouping that is based on other considerations (e.g., interests, learning styles) as well as achievement levels. We also believe that group jumping should be the goal of all group assignments. Like the Boy Scout and Girl Scout merit badge program, the goal should be to demonstrate competency in a skill area, after which the individual moves on to a more advanced level of involvement.

Nongraded instructional grouping and within-classroom cluster grouping

In the Schoolwide Enrichment Model grouping is viewed as a much more flexible (i.e., less permanent) arrangement of students than the frequently unalterable group arrangements that characterize tracking. And although we will present recommendations for various types of instructional and cluster groups, it is important to point out that there are many other factors about grouping that should be taken into consideration in addition to achievement level, and sometimes in place of achievement level. These factors include motivation, general interests (e.g., drama) and specific interests within a general area (e.g., play writing, acting, directing), complementary skills (e.g., an artist who might illustrate the short stories of students in a creative writing group), career aspirations, and even friendships that might help to promote self-concept, self-efficacy, or group harmony. In the real world, which serves as the rationale for many of the procedures that guide the SEM, the most important reason people come together is because they are pursuing a real, common goal. (Issues related to the characteristics of a real problem will be discussed later in this chapter. Suffice it to say at this time that I do not consider teacher-prescribed problems, questions at the eud of the chapter, or worksheet exercises to be real problems.) The major criteria for group effectiveness are commonality of purpose, reciprocal respect and harmony, group and individual progress toward goals, and individual enjoyment and satisfaction. And in most cases, the effectiveness of the group is a function of the different assets that are brought to bear on a mutual purpose. It is these criteria that helped to create the rationale for the enrichment clusters and the enrichment learning and teaching strategies that will be described in a later section of this chapter.

Another factor that should be taken into consideration is the age level of students and the material being taught. Many students begin to fall behind and have difficulty catching up when they are placed in lower level groups. And while nongraded instructional groups and cluster groups within the classroom may be necessary to accommodate varying achievement levels in basic skills, variations in teaching style can also be used to deal with diversity in students' knowledge and skills. In studies of Asian teachers, Steiegler and Stevenson (1991) point out how Asian teachers thrive in the face of diversity and indicate that some teaching practices actually depend on diversity for their effectiveness:

> [Asian teachers] typically use a variety of approaches in their teaching, allowing students who may not understand one approach the opportunity to experience other ways of presenting the material. Explanations by the teacher are interspersed with periods in which children work with concrete materials or struggle to come up with their own solutions to problems. There is continuous change from one mode of presentation, one type of representation, and one teaching method to another. (pp. 196-197)

Steiegler and Stevenson credit the highly skilled professionalism of Asian teachers for their remarkable success and the widespread excellence of their lessons. They also point out that the techniques used by Asian teachers are not foreign or exotic. "In fact, they are the ones often recommended by American educators" (p. 198). Although one of the goals of the SEM is to provide professional training that allows teachers to expand their repertoires of teaching practices, the range of diversity in American schools and our educational traditions will continue to make grouping an issue in school improvement.

Although other modification techniques such as curriculum compacting, which will be described later, are important procedures within the SEM for meeting individual differences in achievement levels, we also recommend that instructional groups be formed within the classroom and across grade levels. There is both research support (Gutiérrez & Slavin, 1992; Kulik, 1992; Rogers, 1991) and a common sense rationale for forming advanced instructional groups for students who are achieving several years above grade level. Two criteria, however, should guide the formation of advanced instructional groups. First, a course description rather than a group label should be used, and the course should be defined by the level of instruction and the amount of material to be covered. This approach avoids the stigma of calling it an honors or gifted group. Defining advanced classes by the level and amount of material ensures that certain predetermined standards will be met, that we will avoid "watering down" the course, and that success in the course is dependent on certain expectations. A detailed description of the amount of material, the rate of coverage, reading and writing assignments, homework expectations, and evaluation criteria should be provided.

The second criterion for advanced instructional groups is that standardized test scores should *not* be a factor in determining admittance. If, after examining the course description and understanding the expectations of the teacher, a student expresses an interest in enrolling, that student should be given an opportunity, regardless of test scores and previous grades. High motivation on the part of a student, coupled with supplementary assistance from a teacher or other adult, may very well enable a lower achieving student to maintain the level of standards that define the course.

A key issue related to this second criterion is that students may volunteer to take a course. Consider the procedure used with Advanced Placement (AP) courses. The content, standards, and examinations are set, but AP is not required. In addition to its attractiveness to some students (and the teachers who offer AP courses), the benefits of such courses are more in the nature of incentives and "bonuses" rather than penalties. Students get course credit for passing an AP course, and there is an additional bonus if they pass the official AP exam at a level that earns them advanced standing in colleges participating in the program.

A good example of how carefully defined standards for rigorously demanding, high level classes can have an impact on at-risk students can be found in the multi-racial San Diego High School. A program based on the International Baccalaureate curriculum was developed at this inner-city school that serves a mainly low-socioeconomic, minority population. Students can select from among nine academic requirements that include traditional courses; an interdisciplinary course in the philosophy of knowledge; participation in a creative, aesthetic, or social service activity; and an extended essay based on independent research. Students' performance is assessed through written and oral examinations that are used worldwide and graded externally; and oral presentations, lab books, portfolios, and research papers are also evaluated externally. Following the inception of the International Baccalaureate Program, the academic performance of all students at San Diego High School improved dramatically, and three years later, 85% of the graduating class went on to college. The school became a "hot" recruiting place for many Ivy League colleges seeking to increase their minority student enrollments.

If we are serious about improving the standards of American education and providing greater access to advanced courses for students who traditionally have been locked into lower tracks, it will also be necessary to concentrate on basic skills achievement at lower grade levels. However, we also need to have alternative routes to advanced courses for those students who have the motivation to enroll but who lack some of the skills necessary for high level instruction. Transitional "prep" or "bridge" classes and individual or small group tutoring are ways of helping motivated students prepare for more advanced classes. These approaches, however, should not fall into the remedial trap (i.e., reverting to the lowest common denominator of a subject area). If, for example, students are preparing for an advanced literature class, the focus should be on literature rather than more practice on grammar or traditional reading instruction.

A good example of what schools can do to facilitate the transition to higher level courses can be found in the Summerbridge Program that was initiated at San Francisco University High School in 1978 and has subsequently spread to numerous schools throughout the country. (Information about this program can be obtained by writing to Summerbridge National, 3101 Washington Street, San Francisco, California 94115.) This program targets talented students with limited educational backgrounds or opportunities who are taught by a faculty composed entirely of high school students or college undergraduates.

The program includes school-year academic coaching classes; an emphasis on critical thinking and experiential or service learning opportunities; year-round family and student advocacy; and many opportunities for students to stay in touch with an active, caring network of directors, mentors, peers, parents, and community contacts. In addition, students are mentored throughout their high school years with close attention and support given to students experiencing academic and personal difficulties. Learning in the program during the middle school years is rigorous and skill-based, emphasizing study skills across the curriculum related to research, public speaking, expository writing, algebra, lab sciences, and foreign languages. Inquiry, curiosity, and independent thinking are emphasized and modeled by directors, staff, and returning students. While programs modeled after Summerbridge may require additional expenditures on the part of school districts, they clearly are a proven way of facilitating the transition to higher level courses for students who otherwise might have difficulty with the material.

Another bridge-type series of programs designed to prepare students for rigorous academic courses in the sciences has been developed by the Scientific Education Research Group (SERG) at Xavier University in New Orleans. (More detail regarding SERG-related activities may be obtained from: Premedical Office, Xavier University, 7325 Palmetto Street, New Orleans, LA 70125.) SERG supports a variety of projects which together form an educational pathway which identifies African American youth with interest and ability in the biomedical sciences while they are in junior high and provides academic support and motivation throughout high school and college until the student obtains admission into a biomedical graduate or professional school. The major activities currently supported by SERG are listed briefly below:

MathStar: A two-week, problem-solving-based summer program to prepare students for their first high school algebra course.

BioStar: A three-week, problem-solving-based summer program to prepare students for their first high school biology course.

ChemStar: A three-week, problem-solving-based summer program to prepare students for their first high school chemistry course.

SOAR (Stress On Analytical Reasoning): A four-week, problem-solving-based high school/college summer program to prepare students for entry into mathematics and science courses at Xavier. SOAR 1 is for students interested in the biomedical sciences (biology, chemistry, medicine, dentistry, pharmacy, and related fields). SOAR 2 is for students interested in mathematics, statistics, computer science, physics, or engineering.

Triple S (Standards with Sympathy in the Sciences): A coordinated effort by the mathematics and science faculty at Xavier to structure basic courses so as to simultaneously maintain high academic standards and provide extensive support for the underprepared. The courses encompassed in the program are the 40 semester hours of mathematics/science normally taken during the freshman and sophomore years by Xavier University students interested in the "biomedical" sciences. The courses are General Biology, General Chemistry, Organic Chemistry, Precalculus/Calculus I, and General Physics (non-Calculus-based).

HCOP/Hughes Biomedical Honor Corps: Xavier's HCOP/Hughes Biomedical Honor Corps is a systematic effort to identify minority students with interest and ability in biomedical science and to provide information about, motivation for, and assistance in gaining entry into a biomedical graduate or professional school.

In addition, SERG has sponsored a number of workshops for faculty and staff from other institutions who seek additional information about the various SERG-sponsored programs.

Managing within-classroom cluster groups

Although the use of cluster grouping within classes is a major improvement over tracking or large group instruction, in practice this approach is usually less effective than it could be because students are often placed in clusters on the basis of a single criterion. In most classrooms that use cluster grouping, all high achieving math students or all low achieving reading students are typically members of the same group. The students within this small group are usually given the same instruction and assignments, despite the fact that high achieving or low achieving students can differ from one another with respect to their strengths and weaknesses within the various strands or subdisciplines in a given subject area.

For example, two students who score in the 95th percentile on the math subtest of a norm-referenced achievement test may be markedly different in their achievement with respect to fractions, decimals, problem solving or measurement skills. One student in the high achieving group may need more help on fractions but less assistance with problem solving. But by using an "average score" to reflect individual achievement in a subject area and grouping students according to this number, we continue to "wash out" the differences between students and within the subject area. When this happens, the potential benefits of small group teaching as a means of maximizing individual student performance are decreased because individual differences between the students and within each of the ability groups are not addressed. As a result, teachers may not see increased achievement for students who were placed in such groups when compared to students who were taught similar objectives through large group instruction. In other words, the use of small groups for instruction will not, in and of itself, guarantee student achievement (Kulik & Kulik, 1987; Slavin, 1987; Walberg, 1984).

The quality of small group instruction depends as much on what goes on within the cluster groups; more specifically, the achievement of students in these groups depends upon the ability of the teacher to group students flexibly and then adapt the learning objectives, the teaching strategies, the modeling activities, the practice materials, and pacing to match the students' needs. Flexible cluster grouping allows students to participate in group instruction when the unit pretesting reveals wide differences among students with regard to mastery of learning objectives for a given unit of study. Once groups of students are formed for instruction, characteristics of individuals comprising the cluster dictate the learning objectives, the type of modeling, the type and amount of practice materials, and the pacing.

Although cluster grouping and concomitant instructional changes represent "common sense" with respect to teaching practices, cluster grouping should not dominate classroom instruction. Instead, a balance between whole-class and cluster grouping is determined by the teacher according to the purpose of instruction and the degree to which students differ with respect to various curricular objectives. Large group activities such as storytelling, discussions, debriefings, class meetings, audio visual aids, visitations, lectures, and demonstrations are used to motivate students, to introduce or extend a curriculum unit, or to teach content or skills that are new for *all* students. Individual or small group activities are used for intensive study or exploration of specific topics within the unit that reflect strong personal interest or when wide differences exist among students with respect to mastery of learning objectives in a given unit of study.

When teachers implement small group instruction, classroom management issues inevitably arise. What will I do with the other students in the room? How will I know they are meaningfully engaged while I am working with the small groups? In the 1950s, the answer to these questions was to assign "seatwork" to the students who were not meeting in a small group. In too many cases, worksheets were used as busy work to fill students' time. This seatwork involved ineffective and uninteresting drill and repetition that bore little resemblance to the way the skills were actually used and applied in real world situations. It is no wonder that the research on this form of small group teaching and practice proved to be no more effective than teaching the same objective to all students in the classroom!

Vygotsky's work (1962) provides a possible solution. He suggests that in order to help all students achieve the greatest amount of learning in a limited amount of instructional time, all students should be able to learn and work within their individual "zone of proximal development." Simply put, Vygotsky believed that it is only when a learner is asked to stretch beyond the comfort of his or her present learning levels that maximum learning will be achieved. In order to accommodate this zone of proximal development, Vygotsky recommended that parents and teachers supply students with scaffolding that supports learners as they attempt the difficult learning objectives that are beyond their grasp. Theoretically, we could place all students in their zone of proximal development if we were able to provide each student with his or her own individual tutor. The tutor would adjust the instruction and the practice activities to suit the learner's next desired level of achievement and provide the scaffolding, in the form of feedback, assistance and monitoring, as the student practices and learns these new objectives. This is the same premise behind the very successful Reading Recovery Program (Clay & Cazden, 1992), a one-on-one approach that is helping so many remedial readers improve their skills in language arts.

A problem arises, however, when we try to provide these same services in classrooms where one teacher is assigned to 25 or more students. Although teachers are unable to act as a private tutor for all of the students in their classes, teachers can increase the amount of time students spend working in their zone of proximal development by increasing the use of small group teaching. Teachers and researchers (Hoover, Sayler, & Feldhusen, 1993) have described the practice of using flexible skill groups in the regular classroom. In these instances, teachers help students in each small group work cooperatively to practice and apply the skill or objective that was the focus of the teacher-led group instruction. By working cooperatively, students provide scaffolding for each other and are not reduced to practicing the kind of repetitive drill that the old "seatwork" approach produced. These cooperative practice groups meet and work with the teacher on a rotating basis; specifically, teachers meet with 2-4 groups a day to evaluate student progress, provide instruction and/or new scaffolding, assess the appropriateness of grouping arrangements, and reassign (e.g., "group jump") students accordingly (see Kierstead, 1985, 1986, for details on managing small group work). This application of cooperative learning principles ensures that all students in a small group are supporting and helping one another *and* that they are all striving to achieve a common objective that is appropriate for *all* group members.

While some students are involved in teacher-directed flexible skill groups, and other students are working cooperatively to extend, practice, or apply the common objective they were taught in their skill groups, still other students can be allowed to use interest centers, learning centers, classroom libraries, software, and technology to pursue individual interests or to extend and enrich a curriculum unit. Students provided with these enrichment options demonstrated mastery of curriculum objectives in the assessment of student knowledge that preceded instruction. Class meetings are used to explain enrichment options and to teach the skills necessary for students to work independently. Student logs can be used to provide the teacher with information about what each student does each day, and contracts can be written by students and teachers, using compromise and consensus, to ensure that each student has a relevant and realistic plan for his or her enrichment time. Of course, teachers can use the enrichment cluster meetings (described later in this chapter) to mentor and facilitate some of these alternative student activities.

Recent research relating to grouping practices and program elimination for high ability students

Kulik (1992) and Rogers (1991) recently completed two meta-analytical studies on the effects of ability grouping on high achieving students. Their conclusions are similar and provide a sound basis for an examination of instructional and ability grouping. The current attention being paid to the elimination of tracking obscures two major issues: tracking and grouping are not the same and what happens within the group (termed curricular adjustment by Kulik) is as essential (if not more essential) than how the group is formed.

According to Kulik's meta-analytic review (1992), some grouping programs have little or no effect on students, others have moderate effects, and still others have large effects. Kulik believes that for talented students, according to his review, enrichment and acceleration have the largest effects on student learning. "In typical evaluation studies, talented students from accelerated classes outperform non-accelerates of the same age and IQ by almost one full year on achievement tests. Talented students from enriched classes outperform initially equivalent students from conventional classes by 4 to 5 months on grade equivalent scales" (1992, p. 6-7). Kulik summarizes the effect of schools eliminating the use of grouped programs: "The damage would be greatest, however, if schools in the name of de-tracking, eliminated enriched and accelerated classes for their brightest learners. The achievement level of such students falls dramatically when they are required to do routine work at a routine pace. No one can be certain that there would be a way to repair the harm that would be done if schools eliminated all programs of acceleration and enrichment" (1992, p. 6-7).

In another recent study, Purcell (1993) examined the perceived effects of the elimination of an enrichment program on the students who had participated in the program. In this study, 19 parents were interviewed and 27 parents completed a survey relating to their perceptions of the effects of program elimination on their children. Ninety-five percent of the parents identified both short and long-term academic and social effects on their children as a result of the elimination. The perceived behavioral outcome of the elimination of the gifted and talented program mentioned most frequently (by over 60% of the parents) was increased boredom with the traditional curriculum.

Concluding thoughts on grouping

It is easy to point out the social consequences of grouping, the grouping practices followed in other nations, and the level of professionalism required for teachers to accommodate the diversity that is always present when two or more students come together. Our schools are a reflection of the society at large and the educational traditions that this society has created. Schools do, indeed, play a role in shaping society; however, they have thus far been an abysmal failure at influencing larger societal issues such as housing, health care, and equal job opportunities. These larger societal issues also are forms of "grouping," which must be addressed at the same time that we struggle with the most equitable forms of grouping that should take place in our schools. Schools cannot shoulder the entire burden of shaping and improving our multicultural society. Until these larger issues are addressed and until dramatic changes take place in the funding of education in the preparation of our teachers, and in creating a national commitment to improve standards for all students, grouping will continue to be a practice that helps to accommodate the broad range of diversity that characterizes our school population. We believe that grouping per se is not the issue. Rather, the issue is what is done within groups, regardless of how they are organized, to help all students maximize their potentials and view learning as both a valuable and enjoyable experience. It is for this reason that the *SEM focuses on the act of learning rather than the types of administrative arrangements that have been offered as school reform paradigms.* By concentrating on what and how we teach, grouping becomes incidental to the overall process of school improvement.

The Schoolwide Enrichment Model

If there is one thing upon which most educational reform leaders agree, it is that remedial models for school improvement have not been highly successful. Attempts to push up achievement test scores from "the bottom" through highly prescriptive mastery learning models have frustrated low achieving students and dragged down the performance of average and high achieving youngsters. An alternative to what one student called the drill-and-kill approach is an enrichment-based model that uses "high-end learning" strategies and accelerated content to improve the performance of all students.

The Schoolwide Enrichment Model (SEM) is a detailed blueprint for total school improvement that is flexible enough to allow each school to develop its own unique program based on local resources, student populations, school leadership dynamics, and faculty strengths and creativity. Although this research-supported model is based on highly successful practices that had their origins in special programs for gifted and talented students, its major goal is to promote both challenging and enjoyable "high-end learning" across the full range of school types, levels, and demographic differences. The model is not intended to replace or minimize existing services to high achieving students. Rather, its purpose is to integrate these services into "a-rising-tide-lifts-all-ships" approach to school improvement and to expand the role of enrichment specialists by having these persons infuse specific practices for high-end learning into the total school program. The Schoolwide Enrichment Model provides educators with the means to:

- develop the talent potentials of young people by systematically assessing their strengths; providing enrichment opportunities, resources, and services to develop these strengths; and using a flexible approach to curricular differentiation and the use of school time.
- improve the academic performance of all students in all areas of the regular curriculum and to blend standard curriculum activities with meaningful enrichment learning.
- promote continuous, reflective, growth-oriented professionalism of school personnel to such an extent that many faculty members emerge as leaders in curriculum and staff development, program planning, etc.

- create a learning community that honors ethnic, gender, and cultural diversity, and promotes mutual respect, democratic principles, and the preservation of the earth's resources.
- implement a collaborative school culture that includes appropriate decision-making opportunities for students, parents, teachers, and administrators.

The Schoolwide Enrichment Model consists of three interacting dimensions (see Figure 1). Two dimensions, called the *organizational components* and the *service delivery components*, are brought to bear on a third dimension, which represents various *school structures* such as the regular curriculum, a variety of enrichment situations, and a continuum

Figure 1—The Schoolwide Enrichment Model

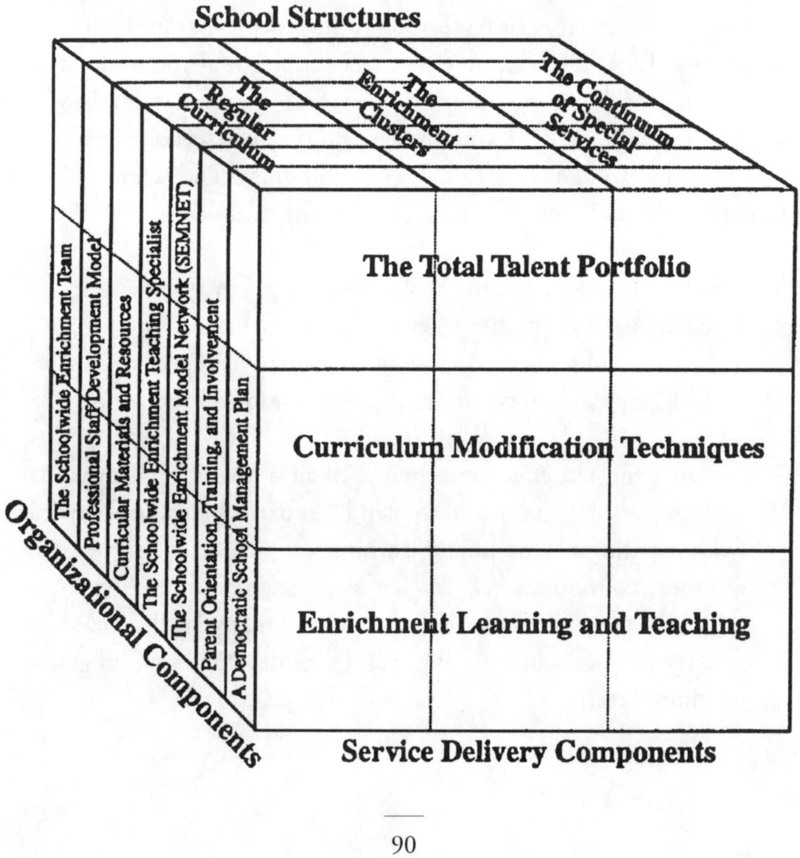

of services that ranges from enrichment in the regular classroom to special projects, internship opportunities, and various grouping arrangements (see Figure 2). The organizational components are resources used to support program development such as staff training materials, an enrichment materials data base, procedures for staff teaming and interaction, and vehicles for promoting parent and community involvement. These components are cross referenced with the following three service delivery components, which are direct services to students and form the centerpiece of the model.

Figure 2—Continuum of Services

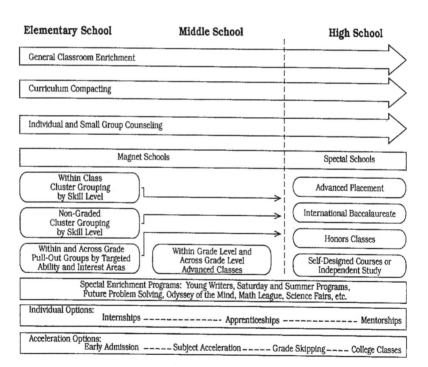

The Total Talent Portfolio (TTP)

This component is a vehicle for systematically gathering, record-ing, and using information about student strengths in three categories — abilities, interests, and learning style preferences. Best-case samples of students' work as well as information resulting from interest and learning styles assessment scales are reviewed and analyzed cooperatively by students and teachers in order to make meaningful decisions about necessary curricular modifications and enrichment opportunities that capitalize on students' strengths and interests. A part of the process involves helping students develop skills for evaluating portfolio items according to their own set of internal criteria and developing procedures for examining portfolio items on the basis of external criteria with teachers and other students. Students should achieve autonomy and ownership of the Total Talent Portfolio (See Figure 3) by assuming

Figure 3—Total Talent Portfolio

Joseph S. Renzulli

Abilities	Interests	Style Preferences			
Maximum Performance Indicators	Interest Areas	Instructional Styles Preferences	Learning Environment Preferences	Thinking Styles Preferences	Expression Style Preferences
Tests •Standardized •Teacher-Made Course Grades Teacher Ratings Product Evaluation •Written •Oral •Visual •Musical •Constructed (Note differences between assigned and self-selected products) Level of Participation in Learning Activities Degree of Interaction With Others Ref: General Tests and Measurements Literature	Fine Arts Crafts Literary Historical Mathematical/Logical Physical Sciences Life Sciences Political/Judicial Athletic/Recreation Marketing/Business Drama/Dance Musical Performance Musical Composition Managerial/Business Photography Film/Video Computers Other (Specify) Ref: Renzulli, 1977b	Recitation & Drill Peer Tutoring Lecture Lecture/Discussion Discussion Guided Independent Study * Learning /Interest Center Simulation, Role Playing, Dramatization, Guided Fantasy Learning Games Replicative Reports or Projects* Investigative Reports or Projects* Unguided Independent Study* Internship* Apprenticeship* *With or without a mentor	Inter/Intra Personal •Self-Oriented •Peer-Oriented •Adult-Oriented •Combined Physical •Sound •Heat •Light •Design •Mobility •Time of Day •Food Intake •Seating Ref: Amabile, 1983; Dunn, Dunn, & Price, 1975; Gardner, 1983	Analytic (School Smart) Synthetic/ Creative (Creative, Inventive) Practical/ Contextual (Street Smart) Legislative Executive Judicial Ref: Sternberg, 1984, 1988, in press	Written Oral Manipulative Discussion Display Dramatization Artistic Graphic Commercial Service Ref: Renzulli & Reis 1985

major responsibility in the selection of items to be included, maintaining and regularly updating the portfolio, and setting personal goals by making decisions about items that they would like to include in the portfolio at some future point in time. Although the teacher should serve as a guide in the portfolio review process (especially with younger students), the ultimate goal is to create autonomy in students by turning control for the management of the portfolio over to them.

Curriculum modification techniques

The second service delivery component of the Schoolwide Enrichment Model consists of a series of techniques that are designed to (a) assess each student's mastery level of regular curricular material, (b) adjust the pace and level of required material to accommodate variations in learning, and (c) provide enrichment and acceleration alternatives for students who have mastered, or can easily master, regular material at a more rapid pace. The first curriculum modification procedure is carried out, for individuals and for small groups of students working at approximately the same level, through a systematic process called curriculum compacting. This three-step process consists of defining the goals and outcomes of a particular unit of study, determining and documenting which students have already mastered most or all of a specified set of learning outcomes (or which students are capable of mastery at an accelerated pace), and providing replacement activities that are pursued during the time gained by compacting the regular curriculum. These options include content acceleration, self-selected individual or group research projects, peer teaching, and a variety of out-of-class or non-school activities. Research on Curriculum Compacting has shown that this process can easily be learned and implemented by teachers at all levels and that students using this process benefit academically.

A second procedure for making adjustments in regular curriculum on a more widespread basis is the examination of textbooks and workbooks in order to determine which parts can be economized upon through the "surgical" removal of excessive practice material. Based on the belief that "less is better" when it comes to promoting greater depth in learning, this process also includes replacement activities in the form of direct teaching of thinking skills and curriculum development options for high-end learning based on the Multiple Menu Model. This model for curriculum differentiation focuses on using representative concepts, themes, patterns, organizing structures, and investigative methodologies to capture the essence of a topic both within traditional domains of knowledge and in interdisciplinary studies. In-depth learning also requires increasingly complex information that moves up the hierarchy of knowledge: from facts to principles, generalizations, and theories. These skills, plus the use of advanced-level knowledge, form the cognitive structures and problem-solving strategies that endure long after students have forgotten the factual material that is the focus of so much traditional learning. The surgical removal of repetitive practice material provides the time for experiences built around prob-lem-based learning, the use of thematic and interdisciplinary units, and a host of other authentic learning experiences.

Enrichment learning and teaching

Enrichment learning and teaching is a systematic set of strategies that is designed to promote active engagement in learning on the parts of both teachers and students. In a certain sense, the approach strives to do everything the opposite from traditional, didactic teaching. Four principles define this concept:

- Each learner is unique. Therefore, all learning experiences must take into account the abilities, interests, and learning styles of the individual.
- Learning is more effective when students enjoy what they are doing. Therefore, learning experiences should be designed and assessed with as much concern for enjoyment as for other goals.
- Learning is more meaningful and enjoyable when content and process are learned within the context of a real problem, when students use authentic methods to address the problem, and when they want to have an impact on a real audience.

- Enrichment learning and teaching focuses on enhancing knowledge and acquiring thinking skills. *Applications* of knowledge and skills must supplement formal instruction.

Many enrichment learning and teaching opportunities are based on the Enrichment Triad Model (Renzulli, 1977) which is one of the most commonly used models for enrichment in the United States (See Figure 4). The Triad Model was designed to encourage creative productivity on the part of young people by exposing them to various topics, areas of interest, and fields of study and to further train them to *apply* advanced content, process-training skills, and methodology training to self-selected areas of interest. Accordingly, three types of enrichment are included in the Enrichment Triad Model.

Figure 4—Enrichment Triad Model

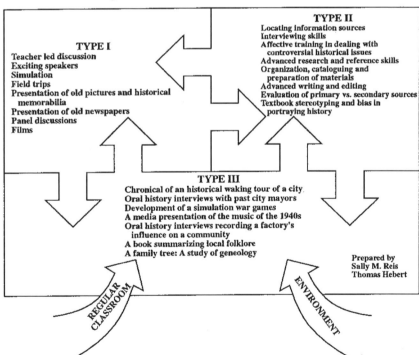

TYPE II
Locating information sources
Interviewing skills
Affective training in dealing with
   controversial historical issues
Advanced research and reference skills
Organization, cataloguing and
   preparation of materials
Advanced writing and editing
Evaluation of primary vs. secondary sources
Textbook stereotyping and bias in
   portraying history

TYPE I
Teacher led discussion
Exciting speakers
Simulation
Field trips
Presentation of old pictures and historical
   memorabilia
Presentation of old newspapers
Panel discussions
Films

TYPE III
Chronical of an historical waking tour of a city
Oral history interviews with past city mayors
Development of a simulation war games
A media presentation of the music of the 1940s
Oral history interviews recording a factory's
   influence on a community
A book summarizing local folklore
A family tree: A study of geneology

Prepared by
Sally M. Reis
Thomas Hebert

REGULAR CLASSROOM

ENVIRONMENT

Type I enrichment is designed to expose students to a wide variety of disciplines, topics, occupations, hobbies, persons, places, and events that would not ordinarily be covered in the regular curriculum. In schools that use this model, an enrichment team consisting of parents, teachers, and students often organizes and plans Type I experiences by contacting speakers; by arranging minicourses, demonstrations, or performances; or by ordering and distributing films, slides, videotapes, or other print or non-print media. The following description from a Schoolwide Enrichment Program provides an example of Type I enrichment:

> Mary Emick visited our school today to explain botany
> with interested primary and intermediate students. She
> discussed the role of a botanist in ecology, biology and
> wildlife management. We learned to recognize a seed
> embryo by dissecting a corn seed and planting the embryo
> in agar. We used iodine to test for the presence of starch–
> the embryo's food–by seeing its absence near the embryo
> (it had been eaten) and its presence farther away from the
> seed. She brought several plant samples and discussed the
> need for sugar and oxygen consumption by these plants in
> order for photosynthesis to occur.

Type II enrichment consists of materials and methods designed to promote the development of thinking and feeling processes. Some Type II enrichment is general – consisting of training in areas such as creative thinking and problem solving, learning how-to-learn skills such as classifying and analyzing data, and of learning advanced reference and communication skills. Type II training, usually carried out both in classrooms and in enrichment programs, includes the development of (a) creative thinking and problem solving, critical thinking, and affective processes; (b) a wide variety of specific learning how-to-learn skills; (c) skills in the appropriate use of advanced-level reference materials; and (d) written, oral, and visual communication skills. Other Type II enrichment is specific, as it cannot be planned in advance and usually involves advanced instruction in an interest area selected by the student. For example, students who became interested in botany after the Type I described above would pursue advanced training in this area by doing advanced reading in botany; compiling, planning and carrying out plant experiments; and learning more advanced methods for those who want to go further.

Type III enrichment occurs when students become interested in pursuing a self-selected area and are willing to commit the time necessary for advanced content acquisition and process training in which they assume the role of a firsthand inquirer. The goals of Type III enrichment include:

- providing opportunities for applying interests, knowledge, creative ideas, and task commitment to a self-selected problem or area of study.

- acquiring advanced level understanding of the knowledge (content) and methodology (process) that are used within particular disciplines, artistic areas of expression, and interdisciplinary studies.

- developing authentic products that are primarily directed toward bringing about a desired impact upon a specified audience.

- developing self-directed learning skills in the areas of planning, organization, resource utilization, time management, decision making, and self-evaluation.

- developing task commitment, self-confidence, and feelings of creative accomplishment.

Several examples of Type III products completed by middle school students are provided in Table 1.

Table 1.
Type III products completed by middle school students

Literary

Literary Magazine
School Newspaper
Collections of local folklore
Puppeteers
Series of books
Greeting cards with original poetry
Comic book series
Calendar book

Children's page in a city newspaper

Historical

Historical monologue
Historical walking tour of a city
Slide/tape presentation of
historical research
Historical board game
Investigation of local elections
Film on historical topic
Archeological dig
Anthropological study
Oral history

Scientific

Science journal
Daily meteorologist posting
weather conditions
Organized tour of a natural history
museum

(Scientific, con't.)

Establishment of a nature walk
Acid rain study
Prolonged experimentation involving
manipulation of variables
Science article submitted to a
national magazine
Science column in newspaper

Mathematical

Editor of computer magazine for
school
Contributor of math puzzles, games,
quizzes for children's sections of
newspapers
Math consultant for a school
Organizer of a math tutoring service
Graphics for films or videos
Programming for computers

Media

Children's radio show
Children's television show
Children's reviews of books, movies
on local news shows
Photo exhibit
Pictorial tour
Photo essay
Slide tape show

Although enrichment learning and teaching can be used in all school structures (e.g., regular curriculum, special groupings, internships), we have found that creating a special "place" in the schedule is the best way to guarantee that every student will have an opportunity to participate in this different approach to learning. The special place is called enrichment clusters. Our experience has shown that implementing these clusters provides immediate visibility to the improvement process and generates a remarkable amount of enthusiasm on the parts of students, teachers, and parents.

Enrichment clusters are *non-graded* groups of students who share common interests, and who come together to pursue these interests during specially designated time blocks usually consisting of one-half day per week. There is one "golden rule" for enrichment clusters: *Everything students do in the cluster is directed toward producing a product or delivering a service for a real-world audience.* This rule forces the issue of learning only relevant content and using only authentic processes within the context of student-selected product or service development activities. All teachers (including music, art, physical education, etc.) are involved in facilitating clusters, and numerous schools using this vehicle have also involved parents and other community resource persons. Adult involvement in any particular cluster should be based on the same type of interest assessment that is used for students in selecting clusters of choice.

Like extracurricular activities and programs such as 4-H and Junior Achievement, the clusters meet at designated times and operate on the assumption that students and teachers (or community resource people) want to be there. The clusters place a premium on the development of higher order thinking skills and the creative and productive application of these skills to real-world situations. Common goals make real cooperatives a necessity, and "divisions of labor" within the clusters allow for differentiated levels of expertise and involvement, varying levels of challenge, and opportunities for different types of leadership to emerge on the parts of students. This type of learning environment is highly supportive of individual differences and, therefore, promotes the development of self-concept, self-efficacy, and positive feelings that result from being a member of a goal-oriented team. To put it another way: *Every child is special if we create conditions in which that child can be a specialist within a specialized group.*

Enrichment clusters revolve around major disciplines, interdisciplinary themes, or cross-disciplinary topics. A theatrical/television production group, for example, might include actors, writers, technical specialists, and costume designers. Clearly, the clusters deal with how-to knowledge, thinking skills, and interpersonal relations that apply in the real world. Student work is directed toward producing a product or service. Instead of lesson plans or unit plans, three key questions guide learning:

- What do people with an interest in this area – for example, filmmaking – do?
- What knowledge, materials, and other resources do we need to authentically complete activities in this area?
- In what ways can we use the product or service to affect the intended audience?

Clusters are offered for an extended time block – usually one-half day per week, and they sometimes continue over several semesters (or even years) if interest remains high and there is a continuous escalation of student engagement and product quality. Students enter a cluster based on interests and other information gleaned from the Total Talent Portfolio. Students who develop a high degree of expertise in a particular area are sometimes asked to serve as an assistant or a facilitator of their own cluster (usually with younger students).

Numerous research studies and field tests in schools with widely varying demographics have yielded both research support and practical suggestions for schools wishing to implement the SEM. Persons interested in implementing this model should contact the authors and/ or examine some of the material mentioned in the reference list at the end of the chapter.

Exemplary middle school programs based on the schoolwide enrichment models

In Yakima, Washington, The Advanced Studies Academy, a public magnet middle school with a diverse student population in grades 6-8, began using The Schoolwide Enrichment Model in 1989. In the

program called The Enrichment Resource Center, various types and
levels of enrichment were provided to students who were identified as
needing curriculum compacting, as well as to other students who were
not identified for services, but became interested in pursuing different
types of enrichment. This program grew out of a gifted pullout program
called the Challenge Program in which identified gifted students
participated for one period a day in independent study activities. The
response to this limited program was extremely positive and caused
both faculty and other students to request additional enrichment
activities. A classroom was converted into an enrichment center within
the school which was staffed by a full-time enrichment specialist. The
responsibilities of this specialist included (a) coordination of classroom
learning objectives with enrichment opportunities, (b) team teaching to
provide enrichment learning strategies in connection with content area
teachers, (c) facilitation of independent and small group studies (Type
III Enrichment), (d) consulting with content area teachers and classroom teachers to provide advice and help in the compacting process and
in replacing curricular content that teachers had eliminated with more
challenging material and with material that students select themselves.
On a regular school day at least 100 students would use the Enrichment
Resource Center for a variety of different enrichment experiences.

One of the most successful parts of The Enrichment Resource
Center was the way in which students who were not identified to
participate in the gifted program could still benefit and participate in
enrichment opportunities. An example of this involved a joint planning
effort between the Enrichment Resource teacher, Bill Gibson, and a
teacher who taught the Challenge Program for identified high achieving
students, Cheryl Kerison. In this joint planning effort involving a
seventh grade science class, the talents of both teachers were used to
enrich the curriculum in life science. In one of these joint initiatives, a
microscope was hooked up to a television and the images from the
microscope were projected on to the screen for the entire class. In
addition, when one student suggested that the microscope images be
videotaped, a VCR was connected to the entire system. This enabled

any absent students to participate in the microscope labs or take the videotape home to work on labs outside of the classroom. Different labs were created, and data collection and analysis opportunities were provided. In one enrichment opportunity, a unit on nutrition enabled students to conduct a study in which they examined their school lunch menus, analyzed them according to nutrition guidelines, and then made suggested changes in the school lunch menus to the school cafeteria director, who then made some of the suggested changes in the school lunch program. This joint planning effort was also extended to the development of student projects. In one Type III study, a sixth grade student named Dusty completed a study of NASA, culminating with an interview with June Scobee, the widow of one of the Challenger astronauts Dick Scobee.

Another innovative implementation of The Schoolwide Enrichment Model occurred in a small city in northwestern Connecticut. The Vogel Middle School faculty worked for many years to develop a resource room component and various content area classes which used enrichment teaching and learning opportunities. A team of content area teachers worked with the Schoolwide Enrichment Specialist to form an Interdisciplinary Planning Team that worked together to develop schoolwide enrichment experiences for the entire middle school population of sixth, seventh, and eighth grade students. These opportunities were provided in schoolwide assemblies, through enrichment speakers in classes based on the model, as well as in heterogeneous classrooms throughout the school. "Lunch bag" seminars were also conducted in which all students were invited to bring their lunch to attend a challenging seminar with an enrichment speaker either from the faculty or the community. The enrichment specialist worked in consultation with all faculty to implement Type I and II activities in all classrooms. This specialist also worked individually with students who wanted to pursue independent or small group studies. One exciting feature of this program was the creation of Triad classes in all content areas. These classes were based on the Enrichment Triad Model and combined compacting, acceleration, and enrichment to offer opportunities for all students who could master the regular curriculum at a faster pace and who also wanted to pursue independent or group research or creative projects.

McDougle Middle School in the Chapel Hill-Carrboro City School System in Chapel Hill, North Carolina, has recently implemented enrichment clusters as one part of their total program for talent development. The cluster program is oriented toward the production of a product or a service that will enable students to learn at the highest possible level, and all clusters are based on the interests of students and cluster facilitators. Clusters met once each week for two hours and each cluster meets for cycles ranging from ten sessions to an entire school year. The clusters involved a visual artists workshop, an actors workshop, a cluster on African American history, entrepreneurship, a software review company, a publishing company, a newspaper for the school, and a talk show for the school. Over thirty clusters were offered to students who first had the opportunity to have their interests assessed. A tally of the interests was provided to staff, parents, and to the students. This information served as the basis for the design of several of the clusters. For example, in sixth grade, the majority of students indicated interests in performing arts, scientific and technical areas, and fine arts. In seventh grade, the majority of students were interested in scientific and technical areas, followed by performing arts, and fine arts. The cluster program, according to feedback provided to the Enrichment Specialist at McDougle Middle School, Julie Dermody, was extremely well received by faculty, parents, and students. It provided enrichment to all students as one component of their enrichment program. Sample descriptions of several of the clusters offered at McDougle School during the 1995 school year are reprinted below:

> Remembering World War II: View the world as it was approximately fifty years ago. Hitler was in power and nations were at war. This cluster will look at the issues of the forties, including the Holocaust and investigate how those events influence our life today. A possible product

could be an archive of video interviews with triangle area Holocaust survivors.

The Actors Workshop: Develop acting skills through scene work from classic and contemporary drama. Actors will explore styles of acting, using works by Shakespeare, Moliere, Chekhov, Tennessee Williams, Arthur Miller, and playwrights selected by the students. Students will read plays and choose scenes for performance-based study. Possible activities include inviting actors to visit, attending rehearsals or productions, selecting and presenting a scene representative of a particular style or period.

Read All About It!: Become involved in McDougle's first school newspaper. Expand your journalism skills as you cover stories for our new publication. Articles may include grade level news, school reports, school interviews, advice columns, selection of student work to highlight, editorials and book/film reviews.

Poets in the House: Use this time to share poetry, your own as well as others. Wide variety of poetry will be included, for example: acrostics, limericks, shape poems, ethnic poetry and choral poems.

The Software Review Company: There is a lot of software available to teachers in all content areas. Which would you recommend the teachers at McDougle purchase? In this cluster you will have a chance to evaluate various software, including multimedia. Your recommendations will be used by the teachers at McDougle.

Why should schools focus on talent development?

Many people view America's public education system as a failed public monopoly. Policy makers, parents, educational leaders, and the corporate and business community are expressing the lowest level of confidence in public education in our nation's history. Many teachers also experience various levels and types of frustration. Consider the following correspondence received from a classroom teacher with 10 years of teaching experience and a graduate degree in education of the gifted and talented:

> My frustration at not being able to adequately challenge the gifted students in my heterogeneous classroom grows each year. With 28 students of varying levels and abilities and special needs, I often find the most neglected are the brightest. Even though I know what to do for these youngsters, I simply do not have the time to provide the differentiated instruction they need and deserve. Instead, my attention shifts, as it has in the past, to the students in my class with special learning problems who are already terribly behind.

Parents of economically disadvantaged youth have all but given up on expectations that schools can improve their children's future, and they have grown weary and suspicious of endless rhetoric and flavor-of-the-month reform initiatives that devour more and more of our limited dollars without producing any noticeable results. It does not take a rocket scientist, or even a person who knows little more than elementary arithmetic, to realize that the billions of federal and state dollars spent on remedial and compensatory education models have not produced achievement gains of any significance.

Lack of confidence in public education is also being expressed by middle class parents who have watched the slow but steady decline of SAT scores at the top-end of the achievement continuum. In an article entitled "The Other Crisis in Our Schools," Singal (1991) documented the effects of what happens when our brightest students get a "dumbed-down" education. "For the first time in the history of our country, the educational skills of one generation will not surpass, will not equal, will not even approach those of their parents. This failure will bring a lower sense of professional fulfillment for our youngsters as they pursue their careers, and will hamper their ability to stay competitive with European and Asian countries" (p. 59). The middle class has become so disenchanted with the quality of public education, that for the first time in history, they are asking for *public* funds to pursue private educational alternatives.

Leon Lederman, the Nobel Prize winning physicist, recently said, "Once upon a time, America sheltered an Einstein, went to the Moon, and gave the world the laser, electronic computer, nylons, television, and the cure for polio. Today we are in the process, albeit unwittingly, of abandoning this leadership role." Every school and classroom in this country has in it young people who are capable of continuing this remarkable tradition. But the tradition will not survive without a national resolve to invest in developing the talent potentials of *all* of our young people. Every school has within it students who possess the highest potential for advanced level learning, creative problem solving, and the motivation to pursue rigorous and rewarding work. And it is our responsibility to make sure that opportunities for this type of challenging work are available in all of our schools. Consider the following letter written by a graduating senior about the importance of having an enrichment program and classes for high achieving students in the school district:

> In my 12 years in school, I have been placed in many 'average' classes – especially up until the junior high school level [where separate classes were available for high achieving students] – in which I have been spit on, ostracized, and verbally abused for doing my homework on a regular basis, for raising my hand in class, and particularly for receiving outstanding grades. (Peters, 1990)

How many middle school students would write the same type of statement if anyone asked them about their experiences? And how many of us take the time to ask? ∎

References

Alexander, W. M., & McEwin, C. K. (1989). *Schools in the middle: Status and progress.* Columbus, OH: National Middle School Association.

Altbach, P. G., Kelly, G. P., Petrie, H. G., & Weis, L. (1991). *Textbooks in American society.* Albany, NY: State University of New York Press.

Archambault, F. X., Westberg, K. L., Brown, S., Hallmark, B. W., Emmons, C., & Zhang, W. (1992). *Regular classroom practices with gifted students: Results of a national survey of classroom teachers* (Research Monograph No. 93102). Storrs, CT: University of Connecticut, The National Research Center on the Gifted and Talented.

Bernstein, H. T. (1985). The new politics of textbook adoption. *Phi Delta Kappan, 66,* 463-466.

Bloom, B. S. (Ed.). (1985). *Developing talent in young people.* New York: Ballantine Books.

Buescher, T. M. (1985). A framework for understanding the social and emotional development of gifted and talented adolescents, *Roeper Review, 8,* 10-15.

Bruns, J. H. (1992). *They can but they don't: Helping students overcome work inhibition.* New York: Viking Penguin.

Cawelti, G. (1988, November). Middle schools a better match with early adolescent needs, ASCD survey finds. *ASCD Curriculum Update,* 1-12.

Carnegie Council on Adolescent Development. (1989). *Turning points: Preparing American youth for the 21st century.* New York: The Carnegie Corporation.

Chall, J. S., & Conrad, S. S. (1991). *Should textbooks challenge students?: The case for easier or harder textbooks.* New York: Teachers College Press.

Clay, M. M., & Cazden, C. B. (1992). A Vygotskian interpretation of reading recovery. In C. B. Cazden (Ed.), *Whole language plus* (pp. 114-135). New York: Teachers College Press.

Cronbach, L. J., & Snow, R. E. (1977). *Aptitudes and instructional methods.* New York: Irvington.

Coleman, M. R., & Gallagher, J. J. (1992). *Middle school survey report: Impact on gifted students.* Chapel Hill, NC: Gifted Education Policy Studies Program.

Epstein, J. L. (1990). What matters in the middle grades - grade span or practices? *Phi Delta Kappan, 71,* 438-444.

Erb, T. O. (1992). Encouraging gifted performance in middle schools. *Midpoints Occasional Papers, 3* (1). Columbus, OH: National Middle School Association.

Erb, T. O., & Doda, N. M. (1989). *Team organization: Promise - practices and possibilities.* Washington, DC: National Education Association.

Flanders, J. R. (1987). How much of the content in mathematics textbooks is new? *Arithmetic Teacher, 35,* 18-23.

Fehrenbach, C. R. (1993). Underachieving gifted students: Intervention programs that work. *Roeper Review, 16,* 88-90.

Gardner, H. (1983). *Frames of mind.* New York: Basic Books.

George, P. (1988). Tracking and ability grouping: Which way for the middle school? *Middle School Journal, 20* (1), 21-28.

George, P. S., & Oldaker, L. (1985a). *Evidence for the middle school.* Columbus, OH: National Middle School Association.

George, P. S., & Oldaker, L. (1985b). A national survey of middle school effectiveness. *Educational Leadership, 43* (4), 79-85.

George, P. S., Stevenson, C., Thomason, J., & Beane, J. (1992). *The middle school and beyond.* Alexandria, VA: Association for Supervision and Curriculum Development.

Grantes, J., Noyce, C., Patterson, F., & Robertson, J. (1961). *The junior high school we need.* Washington, DC: Association for Supervision and Curriculum Development.

Gutiérrez, E., & Slavin R. E. (1992). Nongraded elementary schools. *Review of Education Research, 62,* 333-376.

Hoover. S. M., Sayler, M., & Feldhusen, J. F. (1993). Cluster grouping of gifted students at the elementary level. *Roeper Review, 16,* 13-15.

Janos P. M., & Robinson N. M. (1985). Psychological development in intellectually gifted children. In F. D. Horowitz & M. O'Brien (Eds.), *The gifted and talented: Developmental perspectives* (pp. 149-195). Washington DC: American Psychological Association.

Jones, H. E., & Bayley, N. (1941). The Berkeley growth study. *Child Development, 12*, 167-173.

Kettle, K.E., Renzulli, J.S., & Rizza, M.G. (1998). Exploring student preferences for product development: My way…an expression style instrument. *Gifted Child Quarterly, 42* (1), 49-60.

Kierstead, J. (1985). Direct instruction and experiential approaches: Are they mutually exclusive? *Educational Leadership, 42* (8), 25-30.

Kierstead, J. (1986). How teachers manage individual and small group work in active classrooms. *Educational Leadership, 44* (2), 22-25.

Kirst, M. W. (1982). How to improve schools without spending more money. *Phi Delta Kappan, 64*, 6-8.

Knowlton, S. (1995). Questions about remedial education in a time of budget cuts. *The New York Times Education Report*, New York: The Times, p. 17.

Kulik, J. (1992). *An analysis of the research on ability grouping: Historical and contemporary perspectives.* Storrs, CT: University of Connecticut, The National Research Center on the Gifted and Talented.

Kulik, J. A., & Kulik, C. (1987). Effects of ability grouping on student achievement. *Equity and Excellence, 23* (1-2), 22-30.

Moffitt, T. E., Caspi, A., Harkness, A. R., & Silva, P. A. (1993). The natural history of change in intellectual performance: Who changes: How much: Is it meaningful? *Journal of Child Psychology and Psychiatry, 34*, 152-156.

National Middle School Association. (1992). *This we believe.* Columbus, OH: Author.

National Middle School Association. (1995). *This we believe: Developmentally responsive middle level schools.* Columbus, OH: Author.

Neisser, U. (1979). The concept of intelligence. In R. J. Sternberg & D. K. Detterman (Eds.), *Human intelligence* (pp. 179-189). Norwood, NJ: Ablex.

Oakes, J. (1985). *Keeping track: How many schools structure inequality.* New Haven, CT: Yale University Press.

Peters, P. (1990, July). TAG student defends programs. [Letters to the editor]. *The Register Citizen* (Torrington, CT), p. 10.

Purcell, J. (1993). The effects of the elimination of gifted and talented programs on our most able students and their parents. *Gifted Child Quarterly, 37,* 177-187.

Reis, S. M. (1994). *Evaluation of Vogel Middle School.* Unpublished Manuscript.

Reis, S. M., Burns, D. E., & Renzulli, J. S. (1992). *Curriculum compacting: The complete guide to modifying the regular curriculum for high ability students.* Mansfield Center, CT: Creative Learning Press.

Reis, S. M., Westberg, J., Kulikowich, J., Caillard, F., Hebért, T., Purcell, J. H., Rogers, J., & Plucker, J. (1993). *An Analysis of Curriculum Compacting on Classroom Practices.* Technical Report. Storrs, CT: University of Connecticut, The National Research Center on the Gifted and Talented.

Renzulli, J. S. (1977). *The enrichment triad model: A guide for developing defensible programs for the gifted and talented.* Mansfield Center, CT: Creative Learning Press.

Renzulli, J. S. (1982). What makes the problem real: Stalking the illusive meaning of qualitative differences in gifted education. *Gifted Child Quarterly, 26,* 148-156.

Renzulli, J. S. (1986). The three ring conception of giftedness: A developmental model for creative productivity. In R. J. Sternberg & J. E. Davidson (Eds.), *Conceptions of giftedness* (pp. 53-92). New York: Cambridge University Press.

Renzulli, J.S., & Reis, S.M. (1994). Research related to the schoolwide enrichment model. *Gifted Child Quarterly, 38* (1), 7-20.

Renzulli, J. S., Smith, L. H., & Reis, S. M. (1982). Curriculum compacting: An essential strategy for working with gifted students. *The Elementary School Journal, 82,* 185-194.

Rogers, K. B. (1991). *The relationship of grouping practices to the education of the gifted and talented learner* (Report No. 9101). Storrs, CT: University of Connecticut, The National Research Center on the Gifted and Talented.

Seeley, K. (1988). High ability students at risk. Technical Report. Denver, CO: Colorado Department of Education.

Shore, B., Cornell, R., Robinson, A., & Ward, V. (1991). *Recommended practices in gifted education: Critical analysis.* New York: Teachers College Press.

Singal, D. J. (1991, November). The other crisis in American education. *The Atlantic Monthly, 268* (5), 59-74.

Slavin, R. E. (1987). Ability grouping and student achievement in elementary schools: A best evidence synthesis. *Review of Educational Research, 57,* 293-336.

Slavin, R. E., Madden, N., & Stevens, R. (1990). *Success for all: Effects of variations on duration and resources of a Schoolwide Elementary Restructuring Program.* Report No. 2. Baltimore, MD: Center for Research on Effective Schooling for Disadvantaged Students.

Sternberg, R. J. (1984). Toward a triarchic theory of human intelligence. *Behavioral and Brain Sciences, 7,* 269-316.

Steiegler, J., & Stevenson, H. (1991). How Asian teachers polish each lesson to perfection. *American Educator: The Professional Journal of the American Federation of Teachers, 15* (7) 12-20, 43-47.

Taylor, B. M., & Frye, B. J. (1988). Pretesting: Minimize time spent on skill work for intermediate readers. *The Reading Teacher, 42,* 100-103.

Terman, L. M. (1926). *Genetic studies of genius: Mental and physical of a thousand gifted children* (2nd ed.). Stanford, CA: Stanford University Press.

Thorndike, E. L. (1921). Intelligence and its measurement. *Journal of Educational Psychology 12,* 124-127.

Toepfer, C. F. (1980). *The turn-off syndrome.* Unpublished manuscript available from SUNY Buffalo, New York.

Toepfer, C. (1990). Middle level school grades and program development. *Schools in the middle: A Report on trends and practices.* Reston, VA: National Association of Secondary School Principals.

U.S. Department of Education. (1993). The performance of high ability students in the United States on national and international tests. *Anthology on Gifted and Talented Education.* Washington, DC: Author.

Usiskin, Z. (1987). Why elementary algebra can, should, and must be an eighth-grade course for average students. *Mathematics Teacher, 80,* 428-438.

Vygotsky, L. S. (1962). *Thought and language.* Cambridge, MA: M.I.T. Press.

Walberg, H. J. (1984). Improving the productivity of America's schools. *Educational Leadership, 41* (8), 19-27.

Westberg, K. L., Archambault, F. X., Dobyns, S. M., & Salvin, T. J. (1992). *Technical report: An observational study of instructional and curricular practices used with gifted and talented students in regular classrooms.* Storrs, CT: University of Connecticut, The National Research Center on the Gifted and Talented.

Witty, P. A. (1958). Who are the gifted? In N.B. Henry (Ed.), *Education of the gifted.* Fifty-seventh Yearbook of the National Society for the Study of Education, Part 2. Chicago: University of Chicago Press.

IV

A Second Look at Grouping, the Gifted, and Middle School Education

Paul S. George

*In the twenty-first century, every
young person will be essential;
no individual will be expendable
if our country is to maintain
a dynamic, civil society
and a flourishing economy
in the face of accelerating technological,
demographic, and socioeconomic change.*
— Carnegie Council
on Adolescent Development (1995)

It was a pleasure to read Chapter III written by Joseph Renzulli and Sally Reis, representing as it does, a brave and important contribution to continuing the dialogue that has been tentatively begun between middle school educators and advocates for the gifted. In this chapter I would like to respond to specific aspects of their paper, suggesting where I think we agree and where we do not. I would also like to take this opportunity to speak directly about the heterogeneous classroom, the middle school concept, and what I believe they offer able learners. Finally, I suggest propositions on which I believe agreement is necessary in order for the two groups (middle school educators and advocates for the gifted) to continue to work toward a genuine *rapprochement.*

Areas of Agreement

There are more than just a few places where there appears to be substantial agreement. I think we can agree, for example, that identification procedures for special programs serving students are in need of substantial revision; we appear to agree on the direction that revision should take. I think we can agree that curriculum acceleration, multiage classrooms, interdisciplinary teams, and temporary cluster groupings are acceptable forms of instructional grouping at the middle school level.

I think we can agree that the conceptual shift involved in identifying and developing gifted behaviors, rather than focusing on gifted persons, is a very positive step toward broadening the best aspects of gifted education; such a process will improve the whole middle school by including many more students than are usually served. Moving to the point where educators focus on the development of such behaviors in all students, rather than in just a few, would be even more encouraging. I think we can agree that the Schoolwide Enrichment Model elaborated by Renzulli and Reis is potentially very valuable as a process for eliminating some of the worst abuses of traditional gifted programs; many more than two real school implementation studies are necessary, however, before middle school educators can wholeheartedly embrace it.

I also think we can agree that the most desirable components of the middle school concept are not always part of the daily experience of gifted young adolescent students. I accept that, in their commitment to the success of all students, some middle school educators have created circumstances where advocates of the gifted have a right to be concerned. Some middle school programs may, for example, develop an imbalance that overemphasizes the affective domain at the expense of the cognitive. Gifted students' intellectual needs may, indeed, sometimes suffer during the middle school years if at least equal attention is not given to both the mental and the social-emotional needs of students.

The advisor-advisee program has important goals that middle school educators appear to have been unsuccessful at achieving in practice. Regarding the affective needs of the gifted, in particular, teacher-advisors are sometimes inadequately prepared to deal with the unique needs of the high ability and talented students in that domain. I think we can agree that it is also possible that at least sometimes gifted students are misunderstood by their less successful peers, and that advisory programs have done little to improve the situation. Dealing with failure, managing stress and time, feeling misunderstood by peers, and experiencing boredom with repetitive tasks are examples of student needs that should be, but are often not, dealt with in advisory programs. Improving or eliminating the advisory period is an option middle school educators must accept.

Delivery of differentiated instruction is often spoken of, but too infrequently accomplished, at least in the comprehensive manner middle school educators would wish. Gifted students can then, as Renzulli and Reis argue, be left to languish in classrooms that move too slowly, repeating concepts and skills that the gifted students may have learned even before the first instruction occurred. Cooperative learning, peer tutoring, and other models of instruction, when used ineffectively in middle school, may too often place the gifted student in the role of tutor, giving at least the impression of impeding their academic progress in favor of remediating the slower students.

Concerns related to gifted students can at least appear to parents to be overshadowed by a school staff's well-meaning concern and support for disadvantaged or at-risk students. Cooperative learning can be particularly problematic in this, if it is implemented in a manner that too frequently places gifted students together with others who are slower, less successful, and especially, less motivated to do high quality work. Group grades can, indeed, penalize able, diligent students or force them to do most of the work for the group.

I think we can agree that, too often, middle school teachers are ill-prepared for implementing the very concepts that are touted as effective for gifted students: teaming, advising, instructional differentiation, flexible scheduling, team planning, and integrating the curriculum. University preparation programs and school district professional development have been far from adequate; middle school programs that succeed too often do so in spite of such programs rather than with their assistance. Alas, like other ideals, the middle school concept is too often more praised than practiced.

Areas of Continuing Disagreement

Condemnation of the regular public school classroom.

I have long been perplexed and saddened by the persistent, harshly critical drumbeat of anti-public school rhetoric accompanying statements made by advocates for the education of the gifted. Why do those advocates, even the supposedly most liberal among them, such as Renzulli and Reis, refuse to reject the chorus of reactionary, anti-public school voices in the American discourse on public education? Must a case for the education of the gifted always be erected upon the corpse of the regular public school classroom?

Professors Renzulli and Reis offer yet another reprise of the too-familiar, accusatory litany of anti-public school rhetoric that was heard as far back as Bestor's *Educational Wastelands* (1953), when I was in 7th grade, and has been in the headlines ever since the publication of *A Nation At Risk* (National Commission on Excellence in Education, 1983). Beginning on the first page and extending, unfortunately, until the last paragraph of their chapter, Renzulli and Reis continue their fusillade of negativity about American public schools, especially the regular classroom, and, by extension, the middle school movement.

They make these claims: The regular classroom is incapable of comparing favorably to those of other countries; gifted students under-perform in middle and high school; there is "a clear and present danger facing our schools"; textbooks have all been "dumbed down"; SAT scores are falling; the number of remedial courses in colleges is rising; educators are unjustifiably using educational solutions for social problems; remedial programs have not been successful; America's public education system is a failed public monopoly; Americans are expressing the lowest level of confidence in public education in our nation's history; parents of economically disadvantaged youth have all but given up on expectations that schools can improve their children's future; they (poor folks) have grown "weary and suspicious of endless rhetoric and flavor-of-the-month" reform initiatives; and a number of others.

None of these claims, of course, has been established as indisputable fact; every single one of these assertions has been challenged repeatedly by the scholarship of the *Sandia Report,* the labors of Gerald Bracey in the *Phi Delta Kappan,* and most recently by the work of David Berliner and Bruce Biddle (1995), two of American education's most highly respected researchers. Berliner and Biddle characterize this endless smear attack as the continuation of a "disinformation campaign" that has the destruction of the American public school as its *raison d' etre.*

I am saddened to see this tactic continue unabated and unchallenged, but I think I understand why clinging to it is a such a central, even crucial, part of the current rationale for gifted education. Without establishing the failure of the regular classroom, a plausible rationale for separate and enhanced gifted programs does not exist.

If the regular classroom is a credible educational experience, there is no currently acceptable reason for demanding that gifted and talented students be rescued from it, to be saved for better things. Recall that Renzulli, Reis, and other advocates for the gifted do not suggest that the proper response of the American community to the supposed failures of public schools should be to marshal its courage, make the necessary commitments, and fix what they claim is wrong with the regular classroom or middle school practice. The condemnation of the regular public school classroom is the foundation, the prelude, for the claim that gifted students cannot be well educated there, and must be removed and provided with the best the school has to offer.

I refuse to give silent acceptance to the erroneous claims of the bankruptcy of the regular classroom. I refuse to believe that an adequate rationale for the education of gifted students cannot be developed except on the corpse of the regular classroom. I cannot endorse any proposed *rapprochement* between middle school educators and advocates for the gifted that is built upon acquiescence to what I regard as errant claims.

Any real progress in building bridges between middle school educators and advocates for the gifted must begin with the commitment, by advocates for the gifted, to build their rationale solely on the characteristics and needs of gifted students. Increased collaboration, I believe, will depend upon the willingness of advocates for the gifted to put an end to the argument that current public school programs are so bad that gifted students must be saved from what others must endure. The campaign to destroy public confidence in our schools has been all too successful.

Supposed superiority of Asian teachers.

I can add my own challenge to many of these criticisms, but I will restrict myself to one area, the claim by Renzulli and Reis that Asian teachers have been proven to be more effective than American educators. After studying Japanese secondary education for the last 15 years (George, 1989, 1995), I can unequivocally state that my research experience disconfirms the myth that Japanese teachers, at least, have a special talent or dedication absent from the regular American classroom. They do not "thrive in the face of diversity," since there is virtually no ethnic diversity of any kind present in most Japanese schools; they are, in fact, often racially segregated. Japanese teachers pay little or no attention to any other type of diversity; they do their best to eliminate any vestige of it (George, 1995).

Japanese secondary school teachers, at least, do not use a variety of approaches in their teaching with a "continuous change from one mode of presentation, one type of representation, and one teaching method to another." While Japanese elementary teachers (like their American counterparts) may be more varied in their instructional strategies, the typical Japanese middle and secondary regular classroom teacher (and I have observed hundreds of hours of such instruction) uses one method and one method only – the lecture – over, and over, and over again. Students ask no questions, none at all; so, a teacher often does not know whether or not students have misunderstood. Individualization is unknown; differentiation of instruction is totally absent.

What is correct about Japanese educators is that they explain differences in achievement as the result of differences in effort, not in intellectual gifts, or "lesson-learning abilities" as described by Renzulli and Reis. Japanese educators recoil in disbelief at the idea that a school faculty would use ability grouping or pullout programs that would separate model students, which they would describe as the most diligent, from the rest of the class or school. Therefore, ability grouping and gifted programs are virtually unknown in Japan; and, I suspect, in Asian schools in general. Perhaps we should pay more attention to them after all.

Theory versus practice in gifted education.

Middle schools are, I have agreed, far from perfect; the concept exists far more clearly as aspiration than realization. Dozens of writers (myself included) and just as many state and national commissions have trumpeted this fact for decades. Renzulli and Reis also take pains to portray the worst about the regular middle school classroom. Rarely, however, is the same sort of critical eye brought to an examination of the quality of the average gifted program. Renzulli and Reis claim that the criticism of gifted programs, such as those I and other middle school educators offer, are widely off the mark because we focus our criticism on "an older and more conservative point of view." They charge that our criticism is invalid because it argues "against the restrictive student selection practices that guided identification procedures in the past." The possibility of a gap between more recent statements in the literature of gifted education and the status of gifted programs in many school systems is not mentioned. The fact that new ideas about talent development may not yet have been implemented in many schools is not discussed.

After visiting more than 500 middle level schools in the last 30 years, I am persuaded that the typical, real life, frequently found program for the education of the gifted is far different from the theory and philosophy advocated in the current literature – far different than models espoused by writers such as Renzulli and Reis. In my personal experience, typical programs are too often elitist in their selection practices, blatantly inequitable in their distribution of learning resources, and sometimes illegal. It is the continued existence of such programs, not the philosophy of new possibilities, to which educators must attend.

It may be different in other parts of the country, but in the South where I live and work, I can attest that this is the way too many gifted programs operate. The almost total absence of modern programs for talent development in the middle schools of the South is an outrageous example of how politics influences pedagogy. This situation is not the natural, inevitable, and essential nature of the regular, heterogeneous classroom. It is what happens when the most able, most affluent, and most politically connected students are withdrawn from that regular classroom and when those students and their influential parents magnetically draw along with them all of the resources that make learning happen well.

Education is always, and never more so than in this regard, a complex dance between the pedagogical and the political. It is, at least in the South, too often a dance that the less able, poor, and minority students watch from the wall. In fact, as I write, 30 school districts are being investigated by the Office of Civil Rights in a single southern state for using gifted programs and curriculum tracking in ways that result in resegregation inside schools that have been officially desegregated. Far from what many advocates of the gifted have intended, many gifted programs have become the way in which majority culture parents have secured a quasi-private education for their students inside, and paid for by, public schools.

A principal of a middle school in a large school district in the South, which I believe to be typical, recently said to me that he was under tremendous pressure to open gifted classes to students of affluent parents who did not meet the qualifications of the state department of education. In his school, he said, the enrollments in those programs have led to class sizes much larger than those in the regular classrooms of the school, sometimes as many as 40 students in a class, but parents raised no objection. "They don't care how many students are in the gifted classes," the principal said, "so long as they are predominantly white and middle class." In order to keep these parents from withdrawing their children and sending them to private school, he has often acceded to their demands.

Can it be all that different in other parts of the nation? I would wager that typical pullout programs for the gifted in many other parts of the country too often provide classrooms with remarkably smaller class sizes and incontestably higher status (because of who is in the class) – situations that produce higher levels of time on task, a more positive climate for achievement, higher expectations, the most capable teachers, innovative state of the art instruction, and exposure to a far more rich and robust curriculum. What parents would not want those circumstances for their own children? But, as John Dewey wrote, "What the best and wisest parents want for their own children must be what the community wants for all its children."

When advanced students are pulled out and grouped together, as they are in most programs I have seen, and provided with the best teachers, the best classroom learning climate, the most enriched curriculum, state of the art instruction and learning resources, they may learn more than they otherwise would. Who would not? Under these circumstances, it seems clear, at least to me, that it is not the act of grouping which delivers the benefits, but politically acquired resources devoted to the achievement of a particular group. Can we, middle school educators and advocates of the gifted, speak with one voice in condemnation of such inequities?

We cannot have a new covenant in the presence of schools and classrooms that are organized and operated in ways that produce isolated islands of educational plenty at the cost of creating a sea of discouragement and despair. As John Dewey knew, we cannot have a democratic society that way either.

Yet, like mutely uncritical physicians fearful for their own practices, advocates of the gifted rarely look at the "log in their own eye" before they call attention to the "mote" in other programs. Large grants are solicited and used to study the quality of middle school efforts to serve the gifted; the same resources are never devoted to an examination of the quality of current programs for the gifted and what those programs might do to the overall effectiveness of middle schools in which they are placed.

Supposed inadequacy of American regular classroom teachers.

The constant refrain of advocates for the gifted is that their programs are necessary only because regular classroom teachers are unable or unwilling to respond effectively to the needs of gifted students in those settings (Archambault, Westberg, Brown, Hallmark, Emmons, & Zhang, 1992). My own experience with middle school teachers is different. I find that, confronted with increasingly diverse groups of students in their classrooms, with a correspondingly widening range of achievement, many middle school teachers work diligently at differentiating their instruction within the conventional regular classroom. Many more can do so, given a minimum amount of encouragement and professional development. Confidence in the teaching staff is essential; they are all there is.

Many teachers I observe, and with whom I talk, strive to maintain classroom rigor through high content, high expectations, high challenge, and high support; "dumbing-down" the classroom experience is the last thing on their minds. They are, however, comfortable with traditional teacher-directed instruction and see no reason, or perhaps little opportunity, to develop totally new techniques or methods.

The teachers I observe in heterogeneous classrooms continue to think of the class as a unit; they wish to challenge the most able learners and support the less successful students so that the class as a unit moves forward, together, as fast as is appropriate for the group and the curriculum. Some teachers even compare their roles to the loving shepherd, in classical literature and some contemporary cultures, whose job has been to move a herd of sheep forward at an appropriately rapid pace, while they encourage stragglers to keep up, search for those who stray, and look out for dangers to the progress and safety of all.

Effective Methods That Teachers Are Using Today and Can Use Tomorrow

Other metaphors may be more accurate, but traditional teaching strategies, while old-fashioned, may not necessarily be ineffective. I am convinced, more than ever, that the efforts of middle school educators and advocates for the gifted need to be directed toward making the heterogeneous classroom a place where all students are successful, not toward condemning it and arguing for the removal of the most able learners. I am persuaded that the techniques for doing so are within the grasp of the average teacher. There are a reasonable number of effective strategies that, implemented widely, would make pullout gifted programs unnecessary.

Let me be very practical. What can teachers do, in real world circumstances, to allow the heterogeneous class to challenge all learners and provide support for all to be successful? Most of the techniques that effective teachers use in such circumstances are familiar to many experienced teachers. Among the most commonly used by today's middle school teachers are:

1. **Seating Arrangements.** Effective teachers know that "proximity is accountability" (Jones, 1987) and take great care in planning which students sit where. They understand that sometimes able learners, in their zeal to be noticed and approved by the teacher, try to sit as close as possible, while sometimes at-risk students try to avoid uncomfortable involvement in class activities by sitting as far away from the action as possible. Permitting students to select their own seats will, therefore, sometimes lead to the students who most need to be accountable for classroom involvement being

seated farthest from the teacher. Effective teachers arrange student seating to maximize involvement.

They also organize desks in the room to allow the teachers as much immediate access to students as possible. Desks are arranged so that students focus attention on the teacher's area; seating that allows students to turn their backs on the teacher are not permitted.

2. **Progress-based Grading.** Effective teachers press all students for growth, insisting that each student learn knowledge and skills that are important and new. Grades are assigned on the basis of how much progress a student makes, not solely on the level the student attains. How much a student has grown is important to the grading process. Teachers know that effort, persistence, and motivation are the ultimate keys to lifelong learning and these qualities are strengthened and rewarded in the grading process.

3. **Tiered Assignments**. Effective teachers modify homework and other major and minor assignments to account for the individual skills and abilities of the students involved. Choice is an essential part of assignments that work well in their classes. Different problems may be assigned for homework. Different levels of sophistication or completion may be expected in written work (e.g., essays, reports). Different versions of the same story may be read by students in the same class. Different experiments may be conducted on the same scientific principle.

4. **Challenge Activities**. Like tiered assignments, the teacher arranges for students to work on extra credit problems or other optional assignments designed to challenge all students near their correct level. One math teacher, for example, offers two "Problems of the Week" as a challenge activity on two different levels. She offers a 100-bonus-point problem that requires even the most able learners to "sweat" in the process of solving it. She also offers a 90-bonus-point problem that most of the students in the class can solve with the application of some effort. While students can choose either problem, this teacher's experience is that able

learners will almost always choose the 100-point problem, especially with encouragement from the teacher. Less able students can experience success with the 90-point problem, and enjoy earning almost the same points as other students in the class.

5. **Graphic Organizers**. According to Thompson (Schurr, Thomason, & Thompson, 1995), graphic organizers are supportive tools teachers use to help students organize their thinking, writing, and reporting. Such tools are especially useful for students who are not yet capable of fully abstract, conceptual thinking; graphic organizers can often help these students keep up with the fast pace of the class as a whole. Teachers provide visual outlines, diagrams, grids, webs, ladders, or charts when they present a complex topic to the class as a whole; the graphic organizer is on the overhead or duplicated for every student. One of the most popular organizers is the fishbone diagram, but there are dozens of other appealing images for graphic organizers.

6. **Grading Rubrics**. In the same vein as graphic organizers, a grading rubric brings concreteness to the expectations teachers have for student course outcomes or products. A rubric is a detailed description of what the teacher expects for an assignment, a test, an essay, a product or other outcome in the class. A rubric is a clear target at which the student aims when producing work for the course or class. The teacher will describe, in writing or some other concrete way, the component parts of an assignment that will get an "A," what will bring a "B," and so on. Students who, for example, earn a "D" on a report can look to the scoring rubric for an explanation of what was missing from their report, rather than claiming they did not understand or that the teacher was not fair.

7. **Enrichment Opportunities**. Long before it was called curriculum compacting, effective teachers planned enrichment activities that were extensions of the basic content of the lesson, but in more depth, complexity, creativity, and sophistication for students who

already knew the content of a lesson or who finished learning it faster than others. Such activities are not extra work, which is really punishment, but, as Renzulli and Reis suggest, opportunities to earn time away from restudying what a student already knows, in order to do something that fits their level of achievement and interest. Such activities may not even be graded, unless they are used as a substitute for content the student already knows, content which other students are required to learn while the faster student moves to enrichment in the classroom or elsewhere in the school. There are, of course, hundreds of possibilities in every subject taught in school.

8. **Collaborative Pairs.** Many teachers regularly organize group and independent practice as well as other classroom activity so that it occurs with students working in pairs. Collaborative pairs is a simple combination of cooperative learning and peer tutoring, both of which are clearly related to increased achievement in the heterogeneous classroom (Fogarty, 1990). Typically, a teacher will introduce a new concept or skill followed by whole class work or practice with that concept or skill. Then the teacher will arrange for collaborative pairs to engage in what would otherwise be independent seatwork or practice with the same content.

Collaborative pairs work best, teachers say, when students are paired carefully, according to their achievement or other important criteria. Most often, teachers match a high-achieving student with one who might be moving at an average pace, or a low-achieving student might be paired with a mid-achieving student. Matching high-achieving students with each other is also a way to challenge able learners. Putting two slower students together is often less successful, teachers report.

When students are prompted to engage in "elaborated helping" in collaborative pairs, achievement of all students in the class is likely to be higher. Elaborated helping (Webb & Farivar, 1994) occurs when students are involved in more than just giving the answer to another student. When students explain, persuade, refute, clarify, justify, or otherwise wrestle with a subject together, academic achievement of both members of the pair will often be higher than working alone or in larger groups would provide.

Many different techniques make collaborative learning easy for teachers and students. One teacher provides a collaborative pair "clock" to each student at the beginning of the year – a big, simple clock face on a sheet of paper. Students are asked to make "appointments" with twelve other students in the class—a one o'clock, a two o'clock, etc., and to keep this clock record in their class notebooks. When it is time to work in collaborative pairs or to change them, the teacher makes a comment like "Please work with your six o'clock appointment on this assignment."

9. **Flexible Grouping and Regrouping**. While rigid tracking between classes rarely works for all students, flexible grouping and regrouping within one classroom or among the members of an interdisciplinary team (including cluster grouping) can be an effective way to modify large group instruction. Students might be temporarily grouped within the class or team, based on interests, achievement, skill deficiency, or other criteria. A two-teacher team of middle school teachers, for example, completed a learning unit in which all of the 60 students on the team were grouped heterogeneously and taught with traditional methods. At the conclusion of the two week unit, students were presented with four week-long seminar choices; two seminars were designed to challenge the most able learners, and two were open to all. At the conclusion of this week of seminar work, students returned to the heterogeneous classroom grouping design.

There are many occasions when short-term groups of one kind or another work well. Even in cooperative learning, where heterogeneous groups can work extremely well, there will be occasions when the most able learners in the class can be encouraged to work in their own cooperative groups, permitting other students to assume leadership in the cooperative groups that are formed by the rest of the class.

10. **Study Guides.** Many teachers find that providing written guides for major upcoming tests and assignments helps many students to focus their efforts in productive ways. A one-page study guide provided at the beginning of a curriculum unit, for example, might alert students to the key concepts that will be the focus of the teacher's efforts and later student assessment. A study guide provided during a review for an important test will help raise the achievement of many students.

11. **Questioning Techniques.** Effective teachers often adjust the questions they ask, and the way they ask them, on the basis of the different achievement levels of students in the class (Browne, 1990). With less successful students, teachers can improve achievement during question and answer sessions by:
    - Asking easier questions with a high success rate
    - Working to get *some* response from the student
    - Providing clues, rephrasing, or asking a new question when the student has difficulty
    - Allowing the student to finish a partially correct answer begun by another
    - Asking low cognitive level, short, simple questions
    - Waiting for an answer
    - Letting the slower student volunteer the answer
    - Getting around to everyone, quickly
    - Naming the student before asking the question
    - Asking for their opinion on another's answer.

With gifted students and other able learners, teachers can increase achievement during question and answer sessions by:
    - Asking them more difficult questions
    - Providing them with "positive criticism"
    - Probing their answers for their reasoning
    - Accepting only the precisely correct answer
    - Asking for elaboration and justification
    - Concentrating on higher order thinking skills: analysis, synthesis, and evaluation

- Asking "Why?" and continuing with "What if?"
- Prohibit them from calling out the answer
- Asking the question before naming the student.

12. **Concreteness.** Recognizing that a heterogeneous middle school classroom will contain many students who have not yet moved to a formal operations level of thinking, effective teachers can make their instruction more concrete for learners still in the concrete operations stage. Using graphic organizers and rubrics are examples of this effort. Other techniques used to make lessons more concrete, enabling less mature learners to keep up with others, include using manipulatable materials; real-world problems; frequent demonstrations; use of media and props; displays of key points and terms; many varied, specific, and redundant explanations; marker words (e.g., "Now look carefully at this next word.") and techniques (underlining, highlighting); frequent summaries; and comprehension checks.

13. **Assessment, Test Preparation, and Administration.** Lower-achieving students are often intimidated and discouraged by traditional testing; the most able learners are frequently unchallenged by such tests. Understanding this situation, effective teachers often develop alternative assessments for students to demonstrate what they have learned (Schurr, Thomason, & Thompson, 1995). In many classrooms, for example, students now assemble portfolios to organize a meaningful set of their work that demonstrates their overall effort, progress, and achievement in an area. Other teachers rely much more, than in prior years, on alternatives to testing that build on more than one "intelligence": artwork, notebooks, study cards, exhibits, videotapes, dances, plays, scrapbooks, journals, collections, interviews, artifacts, mobiles, essays, self-assessments, take-home exams, collaborative tests that require both individual and paired answers, experiments, speeches, models, audio tapes, stories, and many others. Any of these items can be contained in portfolios as well.

When traditional testing is appropriate, there are several techniques that lead to greater success for all students, especially in the heterogeneous classroom (Schurr, Thomason, & Thompson, 1995). Here are some testing "Do's" for teachers:

1. Teach test taking skills to the class.
2. Tell the students the purpose of the test, its relevance, and how the results will be used to plan further learning experiences.
3. Tell the students that the test will be difficult, but express confidence in their readiness for it.
4. Cite study references or provide a study guide.
5. Tell students what kind of test items will be included.
6. Provide opportunities for practice with similar items.
7. Set up the classroom ahead of time.
8. Be verbally warm when students arrive for the test.
9. Monitor the testing carefully.
10. After the test, return the results as soon as possible, provide students with feedback about the test, listen to their comments, and use this information in planning future tests.

Here are several testing "Don'ts" that need careful attention:

1. Don't threaten reprisals if the students do poorly on the test.
2. Don't make negative predictions about their performance.
3. Don't mention report cards.
4. Don't post the grades or otherwise publicize who got what grades.
5. Don't express your disappointment with their performance or lecture them about the dire consequences of failure.

All of the above methods are examples of modifications of the traditional teacher-directed, whole-class process. There are, of course, many other methods for adapting that process so that much more differentiation is possible: learning and grading contracts, independent study, learning centers and learning activity packs, case studies, role-playing and simulation, mastery learning, cooperative learning, thematic units, and others. We can agree, I think, that teachers use these methods of differentiating instruction far less frequently than we would like. I hope we can come to agree that it is better for the future of the public school to encourage the use of these methods in heterogeneous classrooms than it is to condemn that classroom and remove the most able learners.

What Can Middle School Do for Gifted Students?

Improving the relationship between middle school educators and advocates for the gifted implies heavy responsibilities for middle school educators. Middle school educators must redouble the effort to ensure that the needs of gifted students can be met within the context of the natural heterogeneous classroom. Simply criticizing the weaknesses of conventional gifted programs, as I and others have often done, is insufficient; middle school educators carry the burden of proving that gifted students can, in fact, be challenged and successful in heterogeneous classrooms.

The heterogeneous middle school classroom

The strengths of the heterogeneous middle school classroom must be established beyond a lamentation on the weaknesses of tracking or a criticism of gifted programs. The heterogeneous middle school classroom should be the preferred learning environment for all students because it exceeds the potential of other models to deliver the common, democratic education our future citizens require. Here, then, are 17 possible reasons to prefer mixed-ability, regular classrooms over homogeneous, tracked, or pullout programs for virtually all students (for elaboration, see Belanca & Swartz, 1993; Oakes, 1985; Page, 1991; Pool & Page, 1995; Sapon-Shevin, 1994; Wheelock, 1992). The heterogeneous classroom offers these advantages:

Democratic environment. The heterogeneous classroom provides a more democratic learning environment. The American public school system has for 200 years attempted to educate pupils in a context in which students studied and learned side-by-side with other students who may be different in their ethnicity, socioeconomic status, or learning capacities. Isolating and segregating learners from one another on the basis of their ability or prior achievement may provide those students with a different intellectual environment, but at the expense of denying them the opportunity to learn within a rich and varying ethnic tapestry that represents our emerging society.

Less labeling and stigma. The heterogeneous classroom offers less risk of labeling or stigmatizing high or low achievers. Three decades of research (e.g., Good and Brophy, 1984) in teacher expectations makes it very clear that grouping students by prior achievement, or by supposed intelligence, can lead to inequities in student opportunity and achievement. Students identified as gifted may develop unrealistic and elitist self-perceptions; students labeled as slow, at-risk, or disadvantaged may lower their personal goals to those they believe to be in line with the labels given to their classes.

Real life. The heterogeneous classroom prepares students for real-life situations. If American citizens are to live and work together in communities characterized by an ever-increasing diversity, educators cannot reasonably deny that experience to young adolescents. Students who never learn to work in school with others who are different from them cannot be expected to work together harmoniously and productively as adults in civic and corporate situations. In a democracy, the school must mirror what we wish the society to become.

Individual differences. The heterogeneous classroom heightens teachers' awareness of individual differences. It may be difficult for some teachers to remember, when confronted with rigidly ability-grouped classes, that even when there are only two students, a range of abilities and interests always exists. Attempting to organize classes so that students are as much alike as possible in their prior achievement may tempt some teachers to ignore important differences in motivation, goals, interests, self-esteem, learning styles, and other relevant factors. When classrooms are designed to include student differences, those differences will be even more obvious to the teacher.

Peer-to-peer learning. The heterogeneous classroom promotes peer-to-peer learning among diverse learners. Realistic, effective, instructional strategies for making differentiated instruction work are readily available. Collaborative pairs, peer tutoring, unit teaching, and cooperative learning are effective ways to increase academic achievement even in classrooms where the range of prior achievement is great (Waxman & Walberg, 1991).

Prevents in-school segregation. The heterogeneous classroom prevents in-school segregation and isolation on racial, ethnic, or social class lines. It is a violation of the 1964 Civil Rights Act for schools to be organized so that classrooms group students along racial lines, whether this is intentional or not. Even if such grouping led to higher academic achievement, the law and Americans' collective moral sense should prevent the use of such strategies. There are many ways to raise academic achievement that educators and parents reject; the racially loaded classroom is one of them.

Fits educational research. The heterogeneous classroom fits with 20 years of educational research on achievement, self-esteem, and education for citizenship. As I pointed out in the earlier chapter, there simply is no evidence that removing students from the regular classroom results in higher academic achievement, unless an inordinate and inequitable amount of a school's resources for learning follow the act of grouping. The self-esteem of gifted students may suffer from constant comparisons to students they encounter in those programs (Marsh, Chessor, Craven, & Roche, 1995). And, surely, it becomes more difficult, if not impossible, to educate students about the fundamental American, democratic principles of equality and equal opportunity when social studies and other classes are grouped by ability and treated differently in many ways.

Effort and persistence. The heterogeneous classroom emphasizes the importance of effort and persistence in success. In Asian cultures, parents and educators offer explanations for student success that refer to hard work and motivation and not to inherent ability. The Japanese are incredulous when told that Americans remove from the regular classroom students who could be important models of achievement and motivation. When many adult Americans were children, they, too, were supplied with a similar rationale for success. Personal success was the result of hard work; America was a society where one could be successful by "pulling oneself up by one's own bootstraps." Americans can avoid organizing classrooms where some students may be led to believe that they do not have to work hard because they have special abilities or where other students believe they need not try at all because they lack those same abilities. The regular, heterogeneous classroom will help us keep the emphasis on effort.

Efficiency. The heterogeneous classroom reduces time, expenditures, and errors related to identification and placement of students. It simply takes much more time and money to develop classrooms where students are grouped so that they are as much alike as possible, and every one of us can tell stories about the colossal errors that still occur every time educators attempt to engage in such identification. It should be obvious that if educators did not attempt to tract students, the costs and errors associated with the process would disappear.

Equity. The heterogeneous classroom facilitates the equitable distribution of teaching talent and other school resources. If, as so many have argued, political power substantially influences pedagogical practices such that advanced classes get far more than their share of a school's resources for learning, eliminating such classes would be a simple way to eliminate such abuses. If we persist in organizing classes in ways that have as much to do with socioeconomic status and ethnicity as they do with prior academic achievement, we will find that the accompanying inequities persist in equal measure.

Differences as assets. The heterogeneous classroom encourages teachers and others to view student differences as assets that strengthen the whole school. Grouping practices that result, even unintentionally, in a hierarchy of classrooms where high level classes are populated by students who are very different in ways that go far beyond prior achievement from the students who are in the average and slower classes tend to reinforce the notion that one kind of student is somehow better than another. The heterogeneous classroom reaffirms that all students are worthy, that none have to be rescued from others.

Average can be special too. The heterogeneous classroom makes "average" students special again. In many states, including my own, funding formulas seem to express the belief that the closer a student is to being average the less money the state believes should be invested in that learner compared to others in the school. Regular classes of "average" students are also viewed as the proper place for "inclusion" of students who have difficulty learning. Gifted classes, on the other hand, are rarely if ever subject to inclusion. In the heterogeneous classroom, average kids can be special.

Rich curriculum for all. The heterogeneous classroom ensures that all students are exposed to whatever complexity-enriched curriculum, and spirited instruction may exist in a middle school. The work of Jeannie Oakes, John Goodlad, and others makes it clear that grouping and tracking lead to classrooms that are markedly different in the quality of the curriculum and the character of the instruction that students experience. Students cannot learn what they are not exposed to. The heterogeneous classroom invites all students to the same educational table.

Social skill development. The heterogeneous classroom provides a real-life laboratory for the development of important interpersonal and social skills essential to success in adult life. Instructional strategies like cooperative learning, unit teaching, and others make it possible for students to learn new social skills while they master new academic content. Few observers of the contemporary American social scene would argue that the next generation needs little work in the area of interpersonal and social skills. Classrooms that encourage such growth must be provided.

Adequate preparation. The heterogeneous classroom increases the likelihood that all students receive the opportunity for adequate preparation for rigorous high school courses and college life. If an important part of the rationale for separating gifted students into isolated pullout programs is that the regular classroom has "dumbed down" the curriculum, does it follow that such a barren curriculum is sufficient for those who are left behind? Or, should our efforts go toward assuring a rich and rigorous curriculum for all students in the same classroom? Equity demands, I think, that educators put an end to any classroom organization that provides a rich and rigorous curriculum for some and only the scraps of that curriculum for others.

Individual development. The heterogeneous classroom maximizes opportunities for individual growth and development. It offers greater opportunity for detecting late developing talent and delays life-limiting choices and decisions about students until all students are more mature. America is the great "second chance" society, and the heterogeneous classroom keeps the school experience from becoming like a tournament where one loss condemns the participant to permanently lower status. The heterogeneous classroom closes the door on no one.

Differentiated instruction. Finally, the heterogeneous classroom encourages, virtually mandates, the development and use of teaching strategies which differentiate instruction and curriculum with the classroom. Tracked classrooms, I believe, can lead teachers to assume that students in a class are at the same level, that they fit into a large and nearly identical group in terms of their readiness to learn. Under such circumstances, should we be surprised that large group, lock-step, teacher-directed, whole class instruction becomes the daily regimen. My own recent observations lead me to believe that this is, with only rare exceptions, also the case in most pullout gifted classrooms. For a whole host of reasons, including the needs of gifted learners who may become the nation's leaders, we must move away from classrooms that encourage teachers to treat students as passive recipients of knowledge through lectures where the notes of the teacher become the notes of the student without passing through the minds of either.

Special benefits to the gifted student

I believe that a case can be made that heterogeneous classrooms hold particular benefits for the most able learners, benefits that would be less available in pullout programs or strictly homogeneous classrooms.

Learning to a level of mastery approaching "automaticity" makes effective acquisition of new skills much more likely. "Over-learning" is not always a bad thing. In the world of music, for example, it is clear that gifted musicians become more proficient through repeated exposure and practice with the same compositions.

When gifted learners engage in "elaborated helping" of other students, it is the able helper who frequently ends up learning more than the student who is thought to be helped. This is not the case, we should point out, when one student simply supplies answers to another. Elaborated helping means that the helper engages in complex explanations, checks the reasoning of others, and views issues from varied perspectives. Helping other students in the class is not always, perhaps rarely, a bad thing for gifted students to do.

Covey (1989), author of the internationally popular *The Seven Habits of Highly Effective People*, strenuously argues that the very best way to make these habits a regular part of one's life is to teach them to others. And, of course, good teachers have known, for decades, of the wisdom in the saying that "You don't learn it until you teach it." The preponderance of recent research in learning confirms the position of "constructivists" who argue that the best learning comes when students build their own mathematics, language skills, or science knowledge.

Gifted learners who are immersed in the life of the regular classroom are likely to realize important gains in peer acceptance and social skills. The long history of "contact theory" in the field of social psychology makes it clear that the more gifted learners interact with others the more all students are likely to think of each other as friends, emphasizing their similarities as persons rather than their differences. In such circumstances, the best kind of interpersonal tolerance flourishes. Other social competencies essential for gifted students (leadership, communication skills, conflict resolution habits, and problem-solving strategies) may find their most fertile soil in regular classrooms.

Recent research indicates that a gifted student's academic self-concept may decline during participation in pullout gifted programs (Marsh, Chessar, Craven, & Roche, 1995). Compared to the self-concept of gifted students in heterogeneous classes, students in pullout gifted programs may suffer from constant comparison of themselves to only the most able learners in the school. Able learners in regular classrooms have a more realistic, and more favorable, picture of themselves as students compared to others. Here, again, the heterogeneous classroom offers special benefits to gifted learners.

There are, then, many good reasons for educators and parents of able learners to prefer the heterogeneous classroom. Middle school educators must be joined by advocates of the gifted in clearly articulating these benefits to parents who may be unaware of the opportunities available to their children in the regular classroom.

The middle school concept

The natural strengths of the middle school concept concerning the education of the gifted, must also be accepted, clarified, and articulated by both groups. I suggest that the middle school concept has a number of special strengths for the education of gifted students upon which we should be able to agree. Regular, effective implementation of these components will, I believe, alleviate much of the need for less desirable alternatives.

1. **Interdisciplinary team organization.** The interdisciplinary team organization provides a far greater range of teacher strengths for meeting the needs of high ability students than a single teacher of the gifted can offer in a pullout program. Even when gifted programs draw off the most talented teacher in a school, it is unlikely that they will be so talented that they can do a better job than four teachers working closely together can do. A team of teachers can come to know the gifted student much more fully, and the constant exchange of information about the students and their instructional and other needs guarantees that each teacher knows the student far better than they could hope to when working alone. The middle school's interdisciplinary team pro-vides a greater likelihood that a gifted student will find a teacher with whom they "connect." It may be the best thing that has even happened to young adolescent gifted students.

2. **Flexible block scheduling.** Flexible block scheduling, exercised by teams of teachers, permits those teachers to group and regroup students for instructional purposes on a daily basis. Gifted students can easily and frequently work with their peers in the sort of cluster grouping Renzulli and Reis admire or with a diverse group when the learning program suggests it. Teachers who come to know the students well can use the schedule for the purpose of adapting to the needs of those students. The combination of the interdisciplinary team organization and the flexible schedule makes pullout programs far less necessary.

3. **Integrated curriculum.** The integrated, thematic curriculum – or even an interdisciplinary curriculum – and flexible scheduling is likely to nurture high level thinking and student creativity while minimizing fragmentation of content. Integrated and interdisci-plinary curriculum units are much more likely to offer gifted students the challenges, the choices, options, and individual opportunities they may need to develop fully. Gifted students who are adept at analysis and synthesis are likely to have the opportu-nity to engage in these processes in a team-taught integrated

curriculum. Unit teaching can provide an astonishing array of varied learning opportunities to gifted students on the team. Opportunities for leadership and followership also abound in such settings. Gifted students, along with others, can participate in the decisions that affect their lives as learners.

4. **Clustering.** A team size of 120-150 students allows for a meaningful number of gifted students to be grouped together for instruction in specific skills or content areas as needed. When as many as ten percent of a team of students is comprised of gifted students, teachers can create seminars, independent study opportunities, contracting, group research, and a host of other truly differentiated experiences for the gifted students on the team, without withdrawing them in a pullout program.

5. **Common team planning periods.** Common team planning periods encourage teachers to focus on the unique needs and characteristics of gifted students on the team. It provides a natural setting for programmatic decisions related to gifted students' social, emotional, intellectual, psychological, and physical needs. Teachers have the time to plan, and if gifted students are present on the team, teachers will have the motivation to plan special experiences which challenge and extend the learning of gifted students.

6. **Parent input.** Teams and common planning time provide the opportunity for parents of the gifted to interact with the teachers of their children in significant ways. Parents of able learners, justifiably eager to access the resources of the school for their child's benefit, can have much greater leverage when they have the opportunity to work with teachers on teams who come knowing and caring about that child more fully than they would when working alone. Interdisciplinary team organization is the ideal school vehicle for accommodating parental interest and influence.

7. **Student-centeredness.** The student-centered philosophy of the middle school serves as an impetus for curriculum planning that is student driven, permitting the characteristics and needs of gifted

children to assume a high priority in teacher planning. Middle school teachers who care about the needs of all students certainly care about the needs of the most able learners on their team. When encouraged and enabled to do so, teams of teachers can be expected to focus much more effectively on the needs of gifted students than they have in the past or than they can when working alone.

8. **Advisory.** The teacher-based advisory program permits teachers to become more familiar and deal more effectively with both the cognitive and the affective needs of gifted children. Teachers who are trained to deal with the affective needs of gifted students can help those students whose drive for perfection may conflict with a desire to be accepted by less driven peers as well as with other affective concerns that may occur more frequently with able learners. Granted, much of the potential for advisory programs to enhance the educational experience of gifted students may remain unfulfilled; if such programs disappear, however, so will the opportunity make them work for able students.

9. **Exploratory curriculum.** Exploratory curriculum allows multi-talented students more opportunities for personal development. Able learners are often interested in a broad range of subjects, but may also need to be encouraged to reach beyond their intellectual prowess. Opportunities to explore foreign languages, technology, art, music, and even family living are occasions to add richness and breadth to the learning experiences of gifted young adolescents that should be valued and protected. Parents of the gifted have an important interest in the enhancement of such curriculum.

10. **Intramural sports.** Intramural sports permits every student to participate successfully in physical activity and to achieve a level of skill and involvement that some academically gifted students might not otherwise achieve. This is not to say that academically gifted students cannot also be talented athletes; it simply guarantees that gifted students, along with others, have the opportunity

to engage in physical activity that is, in a sense, heterogeneously grouped.

There are, then, at least ten reasons why parents and advocates for the gifted should celebrate the success of the middle school concept and guard it for their children. Advocates for the gifted have every reason to be supportive of middle school educators and what the middle school concept is accomplishing. Bashing the regular middle school classroom will, eventually, do great harm to the education of gifted students.

Conclusion

In a recent exploration of the continuing gap between middle school educators and advocates for gifted students held on November 1, 1997, at the annual conference of the National Middle School Association, I asserted that I believed that middle school educators were ready to reach out to advocates for the gifted, ready to develop a new covenant between us. I contended that middle school educators were ready to strike a new agreement that would allow middle school education and education of the gifted to move forward together. There are two important reasons why, in spite of our differences, I remain optimistic that such a new accord is possible – that it is, in fact, essential to our individual missions.

First, the two groups have, in common, powerful adversaries who, I believe, have lost faith in the democratic public school and who seek to nullify the influence of pluralistic public schools on our common lives. I believe that, in addition, at least some proponents of choice, vouchers, charters, and other alternatives to regular public schools are motivated by a desire to completely privatize the education of American citizens. In place of the traditional American public school, I believe our adversaries would be content with private schools for those who are affluent enough to afford them and public pauper schools for those who cannot. If this growing threat to schools as we have know them is successful in any major way, then the missions of middle school educators and of those who seek to broaden the educational basis for talent development will both be irreparably damaged. Therefore, it is not only in our best interests to collaborate, the survival of our mutual missions may depend on it.

Second, middle school educators and advocates for the gifted share an oft-ignored, but fundamental, philosophical basis for their separate missions. Curriculum, instruction, learning styles, and other aspects of education are incidental to both groups. Both programs are, when clearly understood, based solely and solidly on the characteristics and needs of special groups of students. In the case of middle school educators, it is the young adolescent; able learners have been the special focus of advocates of the gifted. Each group cares deeply about and acts as advocates for students whom they believe deserve unique educational treatment that has all too often been absent. A new contract between the two groups can, I am persuaded, be based on these two fundamental commonalities.

Middle school educators must, therefore, work to make sure that the regular, heterogeneous, middle school classroom is, more and more, a place where gifted learners are able to be challenged and enriched. Every component of the middle school concept must be in place in every middle school. Gifted learners in middle schools must be as important as any other group of learners to the educators there. Programmatic imbalances that place affective and social concerns ahead of the cognitive domain must be ended. Middle school educators must redouble their efforts to learn more about the unique characteristics and needs of gifted students and the instructional strategies that will allow those students to grow as they should. We must never, ever, reduce the educational experience of gifted students to that of teacher's assistant, cooperative learning leader, or tutor.

Advocates for the gifted, however, must also bring something to that new covenant, must offer something new and important as a part of the bargain. I believe that offering must be a new willingness to put an end to the constant, harsh, unforgiving, all-too-public attempts to discredit the regular middle school classroom. Any new bond between us will be quickly shattered if gifted educators cannot find a way to build their programs upon any foundation other than the corpse of the heterogeneous middle school classroom. The condemnation of the regular, heterogeneous, middle school classroom by advocates for the gifted must stop.

I believe we can move forward together, but only if we each endorse the spirit of Dewey's remark that "What the best and wisest parents want for their children, must be what the community wants for all its children." ■

References

Archambault, F. X., Westberg, K. L., Brown, S., Hallmark, B. W., Emmons, C., & Zhang, W. (1992). *Regular classroom practices with gifted students: Results of a national survey of classroom teachers* (Research Monograph No. 93102). Storrs, CT: University of Connecticut, The National Research Center on the Gifted and Talented.

Belanca, J., & Swartz, E. (1993). *The challenge of detracking: A collection.* Palatine, IL: IRI/Skylight Publishing, Inc.

Berliner, D. C., & Biddle, B. J. (1995). *The manufactured crisis: Myth, fraud, and the attack on America's public schools.* New York: Addison-Wesley Publishing Company.

Bestor, A. (1953). *Educational wastelands: The retreat from learning in our public schools.* Urbana, IL: University of Illinois Press.

Browne, M. N. (1990). *Asking the right questions: A guide to critical thinking.* Englewood Cliffs, NJ: Prentice-Hall.

Carnegie Council on Adolescent Development (1995). *Great transitions.* New York: Carnegie Corporation of New York.

Covey, S. (1989). *The seven habits of highly effective people.* New York: Simon and Schuster.

Fogarty, R. (1990). *Designs for cooperative interactions.* Palatine, IL: Skylight Publishing , Inc.

George, P. (1989). *The Japanese junior high: A view from the inside.* Columbus, OH: National Middle School Association.

George, P. (1995). *The Japanese secondary school: A closer look.* Columbus, OH: National Middle School Association and The National Association of Secondary School Principals.

Good, T., & Brophy, J. (1984). *Looking in classrooms.* New York, Harper and Row.

Jones, F. J. (1987). *Positive classroom discipline.* New York: McGraw-Hill.

Marsh, H., Chessor, D., Craven, R., & Roche, L. (1995). The effects of gifted and talented programs on academic self-concept: The big fish strikes again. *American Educational Research Journal, 32,* 285-320.

National Commission on Excellence in Education. (1983). *A nation at risk: The imperative for education reform.* Washington, DC: U. S. Government Printing Office.

National Middle School Association (1995). *This we believe: Developmentally responsive middle level schools.* Columbus, OH: Author.

Oakes, J. (1985). *Keeping track: How schools structure inequality.* New Haven: Yale University Press.

Page, R. (1991). *Lower-track classrooms: A curricular and cultural perspective.* New York: Teachers College Press.

Pool, H., & Page, J. (Eds.). (1995). *Beyond tracking.* Bloomington, IN: Phi Delta Kappa.

Sapon-Shevin, M. (1994). *Playing favorites: Gifted education and the disruption of community.* Albany, NY: State University of New York Press.

Schurr, S., Thomason, J., & Thompson, M. (1995). *Teaching at the middle level: A professional's handbook.* Lexington, MA: D.C. Heath.

Waxman, H., & Walberg, H. (1991). *Effective teaching: Current research.* Berkeley, CA: McCutchan Publishing.

Webb, N., & Farivar, S. (1994). Promoting helping behavior in cooperative small groups in middle school mathematics. *American Educational Research Journal, 31,* 369-395.

Wheelock, A. (1992). *Crossing the tracks.* New York: The New Press.

V

What About the Bicycle Riders?

Joseph S. Renzulli
Sally M. Reis

Nobody believes in action any more, so words have become a substitute, all the way up to the top, a substitute for the truth nobody wants to hear because they can't change it, or they'll lose their jobs if they change it, or maybe they simply don't know how to change it.
— John le Carrè
The Russia House

Gifted Programs and the Larger Issues

A good deal of the controversy in this exchange of ideas between George and us is based on one's view of the fundamental sources of power that influence policy making in the field of education. These sources affect the daily work of almost all educational professionals and the students they teach. The first source is "the research," and related issues such as (a) the quality and objectivity of studies used to support or attack particular views and practices, and (b) the role that research actually plays in informed decision making about what will or will not be used to guide educational practices. Because of differences of opinion about interpreting studies related to contested issues, the role of research has direct relevance to our exchange of ideas.

The second source of power for decision making is much more complex, subtle, intriguing, and, we might add, much more interesting

147

to think about and discuss. It deals with personalities, politics, and power in the educational decision-making process; and it is probably the reason why grouping, with its implications for gifted programs, has become the largest and single most controversial issue in American education. Almost all other major issues (e.g., busing, desegregation, voucher plans, state funding formulas, inclusion, class size) are related to this second source of decision making power, which we have chosen to call "the politics of school improvement." We believe that the debate over gifted programs is, in reality, a side show in the larger picture of the current school reform movement that is taking place in American education. We think it can be shown that current attacks on grouping and gifted programs are really a smoke screen to cover up for major failures on the parts of high level policy makers and even some of the reform movement leaders.

However, because of the nature of our task to respond to George's chapter and our different interpretations of research, we will concentrate on directly responding to his four propositions. First, we will briefly discuss the research. Following this discussion, we will present an alternative proposition for each of the four around which George developed his chapter, along with reasons for rejecting his propositions in favor of our own! We will conclude by arguing for a balance of inductive and deductive approaches to instruction. Creating that balance requires general middle school educators to learn from gifted educators how to successfully infuse inductive strategies into the curriculum.

We want to say at the outset that we admire George's enthusiasm for his position and his self-acknowledged characterization of his propositions as "broadsides being fired indiscriminately." This controversy would not be worth writing about or reading about if there were not passion on both sides of the issue. It is our hope that in this chapter we can contribute our enthusiasm for the positions which we take and perhaps even fire a few broadsides of our own.

The research...Whose side is God on?

Research is supposed to be the jewel in the crown of the scientific method and the process by which we can validate good practice and transcend mere opinion when engaging in battles over different points of view. Like the beliefs of all the armies that ever took to the battle-field thinking God was on their side, persons attempting to argue a particular point of view also try to make the case that the research is on their side. There are, obviously, different perspectives about the quality and objectivity of any and all research studies. And if it appears that the research does not support a preferred point of view, a natural reaction is to question the quality and objectivity of a research study or to put a personal spin on it in order to support a predetermined position.

The world of educational research is, admittedly, a quagmire of conflicting claims and counter claims. It is probably for this reason that tradition and momentum rather than research account for the majority of classroom practices. Serious problems get trivialized or blown out of proportion by over-zealous theorists, overblown claims, overheated press coverage, and old fashioned stump orators seeking an issue for which they would like to become the champion. Unfortunately, the policy makers who control our very limited resources are all too willing to make decisions based on whoever shouts the loudest; promises the quickest fix, especially in achievement test scores; or uses the most creative spin doctors! Oftentimes, the validity of information is dwarfed by the zealousness of advocates and the political need to respond quickly to a crisis, whether it be real or perceived. And because educational practitioners (especially teachers and building principals) are too often at the bottom end of the decision-making pipe line, they are often saddled with state policies and regulations based on passion and misinformation rather than scientific findings.

In our earlier chapter we presented research that supports our argument for a variety of differentiated learning opportunities, and we described a research-based model that has helped build bridges between the sides in the long-standing contoversy of equity versus excellence. We stand behind the studies we cited, especially the ones relating to the dumbing down of textbooks and the mismatch between student ability and levels of instruction. But for reasons mentioned above, we will not revisit these studies, introduce any new studies as "surprise witnesses," or even attack the studies that George offers in evidence for his argument against special services for high achieving students. Persons on both sides of these controversies could go round-and-round, and back-and-forth on the research, and still make very little headway so far as the larger issues are concerned. We will, instead, offer some suggestions about another method of analysis that you might use to reflect upon the issues to hopefully take steps in your school or classroom to do the things you think are in the best interests of *all* learners.

The Me-As-Researcher Method

If the experts can look at the same studies and come up with radically different conclusions, how are teachers, administrators, and policy makers supposed to do the things that result in the most appropriate and effective learning experiences for young people?

There is probably only one justifiable answer to this complex question. This answer relates to the ways in which we use our *own* beliefs and experiences to guide the decisions we make about organizing schools and serving young people in our classrooms. We will refer to this approach as the "me-as-researcher" method, and ask you to use your own judgment in determining if George's comments about "wild-eyed inaccuracies," "the lunatic fringe," and "poorly documented arguments" are accurate portrayals of the work of persons who disagree with him. In suggesting the me-as-researcher method we are not discounting the role that formal research should play in decision making. We would, however, encourage you to examine relevant studies in their original rather than summarized or digested forms and to interpret the researchers' conclusions by blending your own experiences with the findings **before** deciding which propositions you support.

George's Proposition One: There is no hard evidence to suggest that gifted and talented [GT] students cannot have virtually all of their reasonable academic needs met in the context of the regular classroom.

Alternative Proposition One
Hard evidence, common sense, and the experiences of classroom teachers and students clearly indicate that some, but not all, of the curricular differentiation necessary to challenge all students can be provided in regular classrooms.

George's first proposition is approached in a curious way. Rather than commenting on *the* most direct "hard evidence" dealing with this topic (See for example, Archambault, Westberg, Brown, Hallmark, Emmons, & Zhang, 1992; Flanders, 1987; Reis, Westberg, Kulikowich, caillard, Hebert, Plucker, Purcell, Rogers, & Smist, 1993; Taylor & Frye, 1988; Usiskin, 1987; Westberg, Archambault, Dobyns, & Salvin, 1992), George chooses to discredit the motives of gifted education advocates. George's argument does not deal with the evidence about levels of challenge in the regular classroom. Rather, he devotes the vast majority of this section to the overall condition of education in America. He spins out a rosy scenario that is intended to prove that regular classrooms can take care of all individual differences and educational needs in all curricular areas and at all times between the opening and closing bells of the school day. It is our guess that most, if not all, professional educators would like to believe that such miracles can be accomplished. But if we take an honest look at today's schools and classrooms, what do we see? Growing diversity among students, larger class sizes, deteriorating buildings, reduced school budgets, changing family patterns, and the social and economic fallout from a rapidly changing society are being dumped on the doorstep of the schools. Teachers constantly describe to us their feelings of fatigue, anxiety, and guilt as they admit that they have become convinced that they cannot and should not be expected to meet the needs of all of their students all of the time. Does George really think we can deal with this diversity by creating an omnibus, one-size-fits-all classroom? It is this approach toward the homogenization of learning, rather than the conservative conspiracy that he describes, that will cause concerned parents to explore voucher programs, home schooling, charter schools, and other alternatives to public education.

That there are differences of opinion about the quality of our schools is not contested. We will attempt to frame the issue by briefly, and we hope objectively, describing these opposing points of view. Following a description of this disparity of opinion, we will offer what is a reasonable way for readers to access their own positions about the status of our schools and the essence of George's Proposition One, which asserts that gifted and talented students can have virtually all of their reasonable academic needs met in the regular classroom.

Gloom and doom vs. the rosy scenario

One side of the issue about the condition of America's schools is represented by the almost ceaseless flow of gloom-and-doom reports which document the low level of quality that characterizes public education. Beginning with *The Nation at Risk* report (National Commission on Excellence in Education, 1983), a seemingly endless number of studies have described negative indicators of the quality of public education. These reports have focused on declining SAT scores, low standards and low state achievement test results, high dropout rates, the poor standing of American students on international comparisons, and the low literacy rates and job preparedness levels of high school graduates. Related studies report on the increased need for remedial courses at the college level, growing numbers of public school teachers who send their own children to private schools, and dramatic increases in the number of persons and groups seeking publicly funded alternatives to public schools. Even George negatively characterizes general education when he refers to gifted programs as "isolated islands in a sea of discouragement and denial." *Turning Points* (Carnegie Council on Adolescent

Development, 1989), a report on education of adolescents by The Carnegie Corporation, which has become a cornerstone of the middle school movement, points out conditions that paint a gloom-and-doom picture:

> [T]he persuasiveness of intellectual underdevelopment strikes at the heart of our nation's future prosperity. American 13-year-olds, for example, are now on average far behind their counterparts in other industrialized nations in mathematics and science achievement. (p. 27)

> A volatile mismatch exists between the organization and curriculum of middle grade schools, and the intellectual, emotional, and interpersonal needs of young adolescents....The ability of young adolescents to cope is often further jeopardized by a middle grade curriculum that assumes a need for an intellectual moratorium during early adolescence. Some educators consider the young adolescent incapable of critical, complex thought during rapid physical and emotional development. Minimal effort, they argue, should be spent to stimulate higher levels of thought and decision making until the youth reaches high school and becomes teachable again. Existing knowledge seriously challenges these assumptions. Yet many middle grade schools fail to recognize or to act on this knowledge.
>
> (p.32)

The gloom-and-doom representation of schools is countered by arguments which portray a much more favorable picture of American public education. This rosy scenario is based on alternative interpretations of studies dealing with international comparisons, SAT test score trends, and other indications of school effectiveness. Drawing upon reviews of research by Bracey, Berliner, and others, George concludes that: "There is no evidence whatsoever of a decline in test scores in American Schools" (p.13); "It is common sense... [that] the United

States lead[s] the world in [mathematics and science as indicated by] scientific publications, patents, and awards" (p. 15); and "There is reason to believe that the Ministry of Education in Japan 'manipulates the test scores' [to make Japanese schools look better]" (p.16). As is the case with the portrayers of gloom-and-doom, certain ironies can be found in the writing of the persons advancing the rosy scenario. Thus, for example, the new bible for the rosy scenario, Berliner and Biddle's (1995) book, *The Manufactured Crisis: Myths, Fraud, and the Attack on America's Public Schools* is liberally punctuated with commentary and out-takes from Kozol's (1991) devastating account of urban schools, *Savage Inequalities*. One would think that if the scenario is as rosy as these authors portray, they would be classifying Kozol's book as another example of "myth and fraud" rather than lionizing it.

In view of different opinions about the quality of our schools, it would be easy for both sides of the argument to reanalyze and reinterpret the studies again and again in an effort to counter the assertions of the opposition. Thus, for example, the gloom-and-doom proponents argue that current high levels of scientific publication are the result of the productivity of persons who went to school in the 1940s and the 1950s, a time when SAT scores were at an all-time high and ability grouping routinely used at all grade levels. A high proportion of present day patents, they would argue, are in fact being awarded to foreigners and non-American corporations. And the rosy scenario proponents argue that while *aggregate* SAT scores have fallen, "it is literally impossible to compute exactly what a difference in aggregate SAT scores means in terms of average numbers of questions answered correctly on the test" (Berliner & Biddle, 1995, pp. 16-17). And so the battle continues and considerable energy is put into defending current practices and collecting more data.

The numbers never lie...or do they?

How can teachers, administrators, and policy makers make informed decisions about educational practices when even the so-called experts draw diametrically different conclusions from the same studies? And when we add the twists and turns that spin doctors place on research findings because of concerns about political correctness and ideological bias, we are left with a situation that makes valid conclusions almost impossible. Without a high degree of expertise in statistical analysis and detailed knowledge about the major studies surrounding a topic such as interpretations of SAT data, it is difficult for anyone to tell what the "numbers" mean, how they were arrived at, and how the data can assist us in our search for the truth.

The me-as-researcher method requires that we address difficult and perplexing questions. Where do the anti-grouping advocates send their own kids to school? What aspirations do they have for their own children? What type of education do you want for your own children? How do you want any form of your children's individuality, whether it be an advanced ability or disability, to be dealt with by the school? We also need to ask high achieving students how they would like their education to be structured. Do they feel that school is a challenging and enriching place? An if so, which experiences make it so? These kinds of questions may be ridiculed by the experts and the stump orators, but we believe that they are as valid a method of inquiry for educational professionals as the barrage of statistics or impassioned rhetoric of persons who want us to think like them. We [the authors] ask you to consider George's proposition about the "hard evidence" in a way that makes sense to you, and to draw your own conclusions about the best ways of meeting the academic needs of all students.

Privilege or Opportunity?

George's Proposition Two: The implementation of gifted programs frequently involves special grouping arrangements which provide GT students with learning privileges which are denied to the other middle school students, depriving these students of their proper share of the resources that the middle school has to offer.

155

Alternative Proposition Two
The implementation of a broad array of differentiated
learning opportunities guarantees that the uniqueness,
individuality, and special needs of *all* middle school students will be honored and respected.

Reductio ad absurdum!

The main difference between the original and alternative propositions is whether or not one views different types of school services as a
privilege or an opportunity. But regardless of the play on words,
differentiated services frequently require special grouping arrangements,
including those cases when group size equals one student. Our position
on the grouping issue has been dealt with in our earlier chapter. We can
only reiterate a strong commitment to the concept of differentiation
and schoolwide enrichment by offering Alternative Proposition Two,
and recognizing and *honoring* that which is undeniable common sense –
that differentiation cannot always be carried out effectively in a homogeneous, one-size-fits-all classroom. This alternative proposition is
consistent with a democratic philosophy of education that is applicable
to all students. And, unlike George's proposition, it can withstand the
logical test of *reductio ad absurdum* (disproving a proposition by
showing the absurdity of its inevitable conclusion). This test asks what
will happen if you carry an idea or principle to its extended extreme.
Let us examine George's proposition with an eye toward *reductio ad
absurdum* in the practical operation of a school.

Consider what a school would be like if it did not have differentiated types of services (including alternative grouping arrangements), if
all resources were equally distributed, or if it followed George's advice
when he says that there seems to be little justification for the existence
of enrichment programs. First, we would have to eliminate all special
education services! This may sound harsh, but these services do cost
more money per student than general allocations. They do require
specially trained personnel, and sometimes special equipment and
facilities, and even special transportation services. Second, we would

156

need to eliminate all sports programs as well as band and chorus programs, because teachers who direct these programs are usually paid extra, special equipment and facilities are used, and students who participate in them are grouped according to special interests and talents. Heaven forbid, they are sometimes even grouped *within* groups! Is it not undemocratic to put all the altos together or, for that matter, all those who play the flute? *Reductio ad absurdum!*

Next to go would be extracurricular activities such as the drama club that our middle school daughter loves so much. In addition to the use of school facilities and access to a "late bus," these students were actually indulged with field trips to theater productions at university and professional stage companies. And speaking of indulgences, what about students in Hartford's Bulkeley High School Russian Club (92 % African American and Hispanic, if you care to raise the question) who were indulged with a three-week trip to Russia (after working all year to earn the money to go) as well as the opportunity to serve as hosts to Russian teenagers visiting the United States. Special learning opportunities and resources? Absolutely! Band, chorus, drama club, and Russian Club are undeniably a differentiated deployment of services, but they are also the special kinds of opportunities that turn schools into inviting and exciting places rather than places that try to force-fit all students into one prescribed curriculum.

"But wait a minute," you might say, "that's *different.* Can't *anyone* join the Russian Club or try out for the chorus?" Of course they can, and this approach to talent development is the fundamental difference between what many present day advocates of gifted education support rather than the restrictive programs that George attacks. We believe, unequivocally, that schools should be places for talent development and that a major goal of education should be to identify and nurture the talents of all of our students. Once again, by substituting the word *opportunity* for privilege, we begin to address the goals we seek to accomplish in schoolwide enrichment, which is based on a continuum of services broad enough to provide special opportunities for most, if not all, students.

The tough questions

Again, you might say, "Yeah, yeah, yeah, but you're still avoiding the tough questions! What about the kids who are just plain smart? Who are not in band, or chorus, or Russian club?" There are, indeed, some "tough" questions that figure into the grouping issue which must be addressed. What do we do with a group of middle school students (within or across grade levels) who are interested in and capable of dealing with calculus or statistics, or who would welcome the opportunity to become involved in a critical analysis of the works of Dostoevsky, Solzhenitsyn, and other Russian writers? Would these be addressed by a middle school curriculum which "assumes a need for an intellectual moratorium during early adolescence" (Carnegie Council on Adolescent Development, 1989). Do not the principles of equality of opportunity and differentiation of learning apply equally to these students as much as they do to kids who kick a soccer ball exceptionally well or sing with perfect pitch? Imagine for a moment that one of these students is *your* son or daughter and apply the me-as-researcher method to the following questions. Would you want him or her to have an opportunity for high levels of challenge in math or literature? To have a feeling of belonging by working with others of similar interest and achievement level? And whom would you want to teach the math or Russian literature group – a teacher assigned at random, or one who has a knowledge and passion for the subject matter that will make the learning experience what one middle school student described as "a small slice of heaven in a generally uninteresting school day?" Does equity go out the window just because these students happen to be different in a high achieving rather than low achieving direction?

Before we even begin to think about means (i.e., *how* will we serve the advanced math or literature groups in our example), we must first answer the tough questions in the previous paragraph. And if the answers to these questions suggest that you do, in fact, support different types of educational experiences to meet the different needs of students, then we can begin to explore a whole range of the ways in which both differentiation and equity can be accomplished. We have offered one such example in our previous chapter that described the Schoolwide Enrichment Model. In that chapter we also described examples of successful bridge programs that have allowed highly motivated but low skills students to gain the background necessary to pursue advanced courses and a college education.

George's second proposition is undoubtedly propelled by the wave of political correctness surrounding concerns about equity in American education. We understand and appreciate his concern for making schools better for all students, and we have offered a concrete plan for doing it. But if we are to give meaning in the form of real school practices to currently popular clichés (e.g., "Success for all" and "All students can learn"), then we must exercise our imaginations far beyond the simplistic solution of doing away with various kinds of grouping practices and offering a one-size-fits-all curriculum. Many persons on both sides of the controversy have agreed that grouping, *per se*, is not the central issue. Rather, what we do with students in a broad variety of instructional settings that will make schools more effective and enjoyable places *is* the issue. To be certain, this challenge is not as rudimentary as the one George proposes, but it holds the promise of making schools into the valued and trusted and joyful places that they should be in the eyes of all students and their parents.

Poisoned Wells and Straw *Persons*

George's Proposition Three: In their eagerness to establish effective programs, some advocates for gifted and talented students have been guilty of less than professional activity in their interpretation of the evidence on middle schools, gifted programs, ability grouping, and the recommendations which they issue for school programs related to that research.

Alternative Proposition Three
You cannot influence those whom you offend!

In our earlier chapter, we discussed the need for a search for solutions rather than drawing rigid battle lines between persons with opposing points of view. The title of this book is, after all, *Dilemmas in Talent Development in the Middle Grades*; and, accordingly, we have tried to keep the emphasis on talent development rather than trashing opposing arguments or the persons who hold them. Our Alternative Proposition Three is simply intended to reemphasize this perspective. Name calling, protestations of unprofessionalism, and accusations about lack of "civic responsibility," "moral obligation," "logic, accuracy, balance, and fairness" remind us of propaganda techniques that are offered as substitutes for research findings, logical analysis, and plain old common sense. George would lead us to believe that all of the research that he cites is "evidence," and that any findings to the contrary are obviously inaccurate, biased, or out of date. Left-handed slaps at America's Ivy League institutions (a propaganda technique called plain folks appeal) ignore the contributions that these research institutions have made to the improved health, economic growth, and quality of life among all of our citizens. George discussed how "America dominates the world in scientific publications, patents, and awards." We are certain that an examination of at least some of the sources of this productivity would lead back to the faculty and graduates of the institutions at which he takes cheap shots. The me-as-researcher method of inquiry asks you to examine the roles that high achieving and highly motivated people have played in the improvement of all walks of life. On an even more personal level, ask yourself what kind of university you would like your own child to attend if she or he were "off-the-scale" in a particular ability.

George's most obvious use of propaganda is a technique called poisoning the well. Just for the fun of it, picture what George would have us believe. In a smoke-filled room, George Bush, Bill Clinton, the governors from the 50 states, and Albert Shanker, president of the

American Federation of Teachers, are gathered around a table with a group of right-wing ideologues. Only a few carefully selected journalists such as the editor of the arch-conservative *Blumenthal Education Letter* have been invited so that the "right" message (no pun intended) will get out to parents of the gifted and the public in general. We note, of course, that the group includes both Democrats and Republicans, liberals and conservatives. But regardless of these persons' political persuasions, the agenda of this unlikely alliance is to do one and only one thing – conspire to destroy America's system of free public education and replace it with a voucher system "in order to justify the removal of gifted and talented learners from the mainstream regular classroom to support the creation of privileged, miniature private academies within the public schools" (p. 23). We believe that George's conspiracy theory might be the stuff out of which fiction is made, but in order to even fictionalize such nonsense, he will first have to unravel a few logistical problems.

First, why would politicians, who are mainly concerned with delivering *good* news and appealing to a *majority* of voters, suppress reports about school success such as the *Sandia Report*, and why would they place their political careers on the line for the benefit of an extremely small percentage of our nation's school children? Politicians woo majorities because that is the way they can be re-elected. Political support for gifted programs has, in fact, been very limited. In the very best of times, advocates for gifted education have only been able to gain appropriations of less that one-half of one percent of state educational moneys; and at the federal level, appropriations have been so small as to appear only as an asterisk in the federal budget. Compare these figures with the billions of state and federal dollars that have been allocated for compensatory programs. You do not need to be a rocket scientist to see how and where the politicians have invested their energy and their money.

Second, programs for the gifted and talented, with their emphasis on creative and critical thinking, have actually been on the "hit lists" of political conservatives because, heaven forbid, such programs might teach young people to think for themselves. For example, the American Family Association of Arkansas, a conservative parent group, recently led a vigorous campaign to close down the Governor's School of Arkansas (a summer program for academically and artistically talented students) because, they said, "it was anti-Christian and a tool for brainwashing" (Governor's School, 1995).

Third, George further attempts to poison the well by trying to create relationships between what he calls "the lunatic fringe," the *Blumenthal Education Letter*, and persons advocating programs for the gifted. Because we [the authors] are associated with the National Research Center on the Gifted and Talented, we receive virtually every publication in the field and every syndicated news article (through our university's news clipping service) that discusses programs and issues related to gifted education. We have never seen or heard of the *Blumenthal Education Letter* until reading George's chapter. But once again, we ask that you apply the me-as-researcher technique. Have you ever seen this newsletter floating around your school or district? Have any items from it been reproduced in local newspapers, gifted program documents, or literature circulated by parent advocacy groups? Are the parents who advocate for gifted programs, or any aspect of high quality education for that matter, associated with only one political party? If the answers to any of these questions is no, than the me-as-researcher method of analysis must lead you to conclude that George is, indeed, poisoning the well.

Finally, the poisoning the well technique can also be seen in George's off-handed remarks about how gifted advocates "mock" the personal and social concerns of young adolescents, how they are insensitive to desegration, the eradication of poverty, the disintegration of cities, the development of community and unity, and other concerns related to moral obligation and civic responsibility. (An interest in personal and social development as well as other societal issues is reflected in these divisions of the National Association for Gifted Children: Counseling and Guidance, Early childhood, Future Studies, Global Awareness, Special Populations, and Parent and Community Divisions. It is also worth mentioning that one of only four Position Papers published by this organization deals with personal and social development.) At the risk of being obstreperous, we are surprised he did not add damage to the rain forests and depletion of the ozone layer to his list! These important societal issues should be everyone's concern, but to place the responsibility on one group simply because their advocacy efforts are focused elsewhere is nothing short of deceit and quackery. *Every* individual and group prioritizes the areas in which they work and to which they will devote their time and energy. George's poisoning the well tactic regarding these larger societal issues could be applied to almost any individual or group that is not "out there" on the barricades fighting to reverse every societal impairment. Each of us, including George, must examine his or her own priorities and commitments and ask ourselves when is the last time we "marched" for one of the issues mentioned above. And if the answer is not recently, and not very often, then waving the flag about these larger societal issues is merely a smoke screen to divert attention away from the heart and soul of what education is all about – effective and enjoyable learning for all students, *including* high as well as average and low achieving young people. The me-as-researcher method of analysis asks the reader to use his or her own judgment about whether or not these larger societal issues can be blamed on gifted program advocates, or are they part of a poisoning the well strategy? Each person must examine his or her own positions, values, and actions as well as those of the people we know and with whom we work.

George comments: "Some of the more extremist advocates for the gifted set up 'straw man' arguments that the most inexperienced freshman debater would recognize as illogical and unprofessional." Needless to say, extremism in *any* form should always be questioned. But truly experienced debaters recognize that extremism, by definition, does not represent the mainstream position on anything, otherwise it would not be extreme. When George uses an attack on extreme positions as the centerpiece of his argument, we must raise the question: Who is setting up a straw man? We [the authors] and the majority of present-day leaders in our field support what is today a much more flexible, inclusive, and accepted approach to differentiation and talent development. George's attack on present-day mainstream thought would be akin to us writing an article that treated today's middle schools as if they were still junior high schools. The orientation toward middle level education has changed and so has the orientation toward developing the gifts and talents of young people.

And the present-day orientation about a broader approach to talent development is not exactly new. Our article entitled "What Makes Giftedness? Reexamining a Definition" (Renzulli, 1978), the most widely cited publication in the field, is 20 years old. And when George says that the field is insensitive to minorities, and has only recently addressed minority group concerns, we remind the reader that articles such as "Talent Potential in Minority Group Students" (Renzulli, 1973) appeared a quarter century ago. A creditable examination of the literature and the history of the gifted education movement will reveal that numerous publications, conferences, and symposia have been devoted entirely to broadened conceptions of giftedness and multicultural populations. In our current work at the National Research Center on the Gifted and Talented, the Absolute [Federal] Priority Number 1 that guides our research is a focus on the full range of at-risk students. If gifted programs are the subversive agenda of conservative forces in government, we wonder how this priority about at-risk populations sneaked through the agenda of the hypothetical meeting in the smoke-filled room mentioned above!

We are not arguing that restrictive practices have never been a part of the history of gifted education or that some persons in the field do not continue to support more restrictive ideologies. Nor do we disagree that some state guidelines for gifted programs lag behind contemporary research and recommended programming practices. But this situation, which is not unique to the gifted education field, is almost always the case when there is a research-into-practice gap. But an examination of state regulations and guidelines reveals that major changes are taking place at the state level and that the trend is decidedly toward more flexible and inclusive approaches to talent development. New guidelines for identification have been introduced in some states, and other states have introduced waivers and alternative procedures to promote the inclusion of more diversified types of talents and members of traditionally overlooked groups. Just when major strides are being achieved in more diversified approaches to differentiation and inclusion, stump orators, persons with their own axes to grind, and those who want to explain away a general dissatisfaction with the quality of our nation's schools seem to want to blame everything on "the gifted." Throwing out the baby with the bath water has never been a solution for making anything better. We refer you once again to the sections about the secret laboratories of school improvement and broadened conceptions of giftedness discussed in our earlier chapter. If George and other critics of gifted programs care about developing the talents of all of America's youth, then their lofty alarm and impressive energy would be greatly appreciated in building rather than attempting to destroy a very delicate but creative and well-intentioned component of American education.

> *George's Proposition Four: Educators have more urgent concerns which require the concerted energy and commitment of all of us.*

> **Alternative Proposition Four**
> **The most urgent concern of educators is to make each learning experience for each and every student as enjoyable, exciting, rewarding, and as valuable as it can be.**

In the previous section, we discussed the larger societal issues that George is alluding to when he talks about the "more urgent concerns" in his fourth proposition. The most urgent concerns of teachers and administrators are the ways in which we can deliver enjoyable and effective learning because that is the domain over which we have the most immediate influence. This influence is manifested mainly in our daily work, but we also believe that practitioners must become more politically active and responsible for guiding the kinds of decisions that affect our daily work. We will discuss ways of pursuing this responsibility in the final section of this chapter. At this time, suffice it to say that there is nothing more urgent than developing the gifts and talents of all children to the highest levels possible. These gifts and talents are our country's greatest natural resources. Good schools may not be powerful enough to correct society's ills, but if we do an effective job in our schools and classrooms, we as educators will contribute our fair share to the urgent concerns of societal improvement.

To be painfully frank, we thought that George might be using hyperbole in the discussion of his fourth proposition. Is he serious when he argues *for* "a uniform education" for everyone and *against* trying to "educate every student to the limits of his or her ability?" Or when he writes that "asking the schools to organize and operate so as to provide enrichment or acceleration beyond a curriculum which provides a uniform education may be *unconstitutional?*" (pp. 33-34, italics added). We are reminded of the following excerpt from Kurt Vonnegut's short story entitled "Harrison Bergeron" (Vonnegut, 1968):

> The year was 2081, and everybody was finally equal. They weren't only equal before God and the law. They were equal every which way. Nobody was smarter than anyone else. Nobody was better looking than anyone else. Nobody was stronger or quicker than anybody else. All this equality was due to the 211th, 212th, and 213th Amendments to the Constitution, and the unceasing vigilance of agents of the United States Handicapper General. (p.55)

So begins a story that tells about smart people who are required to wear electronic devices to keep them from thinking faster or better than others; about outstanding dancers who are required to attach sandbags to their ankles so that they will not excel above the "universal standard" set by the Handicapper General's office, and other forms of government control designed to keep everybody equal. We should keep Vonnegut's allegory in mind as we think about the implications of declaring enrichment and acceleration to be unconstitutional or arguing that the state is only allowed to provide a uniform education to all of its citizens.

Education in a democracy should serve as *the* primary source for liberating the mind and advancing knowledge, motivation, and the creative spirit that will result in the continuous improvement of the human condition. We do not disagree with George when he describes rampant present-day problems such as teenage pregnancy, high dropout rates, and growing poverty rates among children. And we also agree that all children deserve a quality education and that we should devote our attention and energy to these problems. But we fail to see a connection between these needs and George's arguments for "a uniform education" and for the elimination of programs that challenge high achieving students. In many cases these programs are a saving grace in areas that serve poor youngsters: what one urban educator described as "an academic way out" that is equivalent to how basketball serves as a higher education vehicle for gifted athletes. And finally, speaking of ways out, how will our society find the people who are capable of solving some of the pressing problems George mentions, as well as a host of other medical, nutritional, environmental, social, and economic problems, if we do not devote time to developing the talents of our young people? There is nothing more valuable nor important to our nation, and all the nations of the world, than the vast talent potentials of our young people. These potentials are the world's most valuable and renewable natural resource. When we even flirt with recommendations about "a uniform education" and doing away with enriched and accelerated learning, then Kurt Vonnegut's Handicapper General might already be here, disguised as a thing we call our public school system.

Avoiding the Handicapper General by Balancing Deductive with Inductive Approaches to Learning

We believe that enrichment teaching and learning may be a successful alternative for the development of talents in our students. We will argue, however, that in spite of all that has been written, every theory of teaching and learning can be classified into one of two general models.

There are, obviously, occasions when a particular approach transcends both models; however, for purposes of clarifying the main features of enrichment learning and teaching, we will treat the two main models as polar opposites. Both models of learning and teaching are valuable in the overall process of schooling, and a well-balanced school program must make use of both of these general approaches to learning and teaching.

Although many names have been used to describe the two models that will be discussed, we will simply refer to them as the Deductive Model and the Inductive Model. The Deductive Model is the one with which most educators are familiar and the one that has guided the overwhelming majority of what takes place in classrooms and other places where formal learning is pursued. The Inductive Model, on the other hand, represents the kinds of learning that take place outside of formal school situations. A good way to understand the difference between these two types of learning is to compare how learning takes place in a typical classroom with how someone might learn new material or skills in real world situations. Classrooms are characterized by relatively fixed time schedules, segmented subjects or topics, predetermined sets of information and activity, tests and grades to determine progress, and a pattern of organization that is largely driven by the need to acquire and assimilate information and skills imposed from above and from outside the classroom. The major assumption in the deductive model is that current learning will have transfer value for some future problem, course, occupational pursuit, or life activity.

Contrast this type of learning with the more natural chain of events that takes place in inductive situations such as a research laboratory, business office, or film studio. The goal in these situations is to produce a product or service. All resources, information, schedules, and sequences of events are directed toward this goal, and evaluation and assessment (rather than grading) is a function of the quality of the product or service as viewed through the eyes of a client or consumer. For example, everything that results in learning in a research laboratory is for present use; and, therefore, looking up new information, conducting an experiment, analyzing results, or preparing a report is focused primarily on the present rather than the future. Even the amount of time devoted to a particular project cannot be determined in advance because the nature of the problem and the unknown obstacles that might be encountered prevent us from prescribing rigid schedules.

The deductive model has dominated the ways in which most formal education is pursued, and the "track record" of the model has been less than impressive. One need only reflect for a moment on his or her own school experience to realize that with the exception of basic language and arithmetic, much of the compartmentalized material learned for some remote and ambiguous future situation is seldom used in the conduct of daily activities. The names of famous generals, the geometric formulas, the periodic table, and the parts of a plant are quickly forgotten; and even if remembered, they do not have direct applicability to the problems that most people encounter in their daily lives. This is not to say that previously learned information is unimportant, but its relevance, meaningfulness, and endurance for future use is minimized when it is almost always learned apart from real life situations.

Deductive learning is based mainly on the factory model or human engineering conception of schooling which has developed around inflexible schedules that fit into the school day rather than the ideal conditions for teaching and learning. The underlying psychological theory is behaviorism, and the central concept of this ideology is that schools should prepare young people for smooth adjustment into the culture and work force of the society at large. A curriculum based on deductive learning must be examined in terms of both what is taught and how it is taught. The issue of what is (or should be) taught has always been the subject of controversy, ranging from a conservative position that emphasizes a classical or basic education curriculum to a more liberal perspective that includes contemporary knowledge and life adjustment experiences (e.g., driver education, sex education, computer literacy). By and large, American schools have tried to adapt what is taught to changes taking place in our society. Recent concerns about the kinds of skills that will be required in a rapidly changing job market have accelerated curricular changes that will prepare students for careers in technological fields and what has been described as a post-industrial society. Nowhere is this change more evident than in the emphasis that is being placed currently on thinking skills and interdisciplinary approaches to curriculum. These changes are viewed as favorable developments so far as schoolwide enrichment is concerned; however, the deductive model still places limitations on learning because of restrictions on *how* material is taught.

Although most schools have introduced teaching techniques that go beyond traditional drill and recitation, the predominant instructional model continues to be a prescribed and presented approach to learning. The teacher, textbook, or curriculum guide prescribes what is to be taught, and the material is presented to students in a predetermined manner. Educators have become more clever and imaginative in the teaching models employed, and it is not uncommon to see teachers using approaches such as discovery learning, simulations, cooperative learning, inquiry training, problem-centered learning, concept learning, and a host of variations on these basic models. More recent approaches include simulated problem solving through the use of interactive video discs and computer programs. Some of these approaches certainly make learning more active and enjoyable than traditional, content-based deductive learning, but the "bottom line" is that there are certain predetermined bodies of information and thinking processes that students are expected to acquire. The instructional effects of the deductive model are those directly achieved by leading the learner in prescribed directions. As indicated above, there is nothing inherently "wrong" with the deductive model; however, it is based on a limited conception of the role of the learner. It fails to consider variations in interests and learning styles, and it always places students in roles of lesson learners and exercise doers rather than authentic, first-hand inquirers. There is also no inherent value in doing things the way they have always been done, for little progress would ever be made if we continued to follow that mindset.

Inductive learning, on the other hand, focuses on the *present use* of content and processes as a way of integrating material and thinking skills into the more enduring structure of the learner's repertoire. And it is these more enduring structures that have the greatest amount of transfer value for future use. When content and processes are learned in authentic, contextual situations, they result in more meaningful uses of information and problem solving strategies than the learning that takes place in artificial, preparation-for-the-future situations. If persons involved in inductive learning experiences are given some choice in the domains and activities in which they are engaged, and if present experience is directed toward realistic and personalized goals, this type of learning creates its own relevancy and meaningfulness. This type of education focuses on creative productivity and learning how-to-learn skills and will complement our move toward a new century in which constant change may be the nature of life.

If we agree that people do learn when they are outside of schools and classrooms, in the "real world" as it is sometimes called, then we need to examine the dimensions of this type of learning and the ways that real world learning can be brought into the school. But we must also be extremely cautious whenever we think about bringing anything into the school. Our track record in this regard has been one of structuring and institutionalizing even the most innovative approaches to learning. We recall how the much heralded concept of Discovery Learning ended up being what a colleague called "sneaky telling" in which teachers waited until students "discovered" the answer that the teacher had been waiting for. We also recall how a focus on thinking skills and creative thinking fell prey to the same types of formulas and prescribed activities that characterized the content-based curriculum which has been criticized so strongly by thinking skills advocates. Even our present fascination with computers and video discs is, in some cases, turning out to be little more than "electronic worksheets."

The type of enrichment learning and teaching mentioned in our earlier chapter is essentially an inductive approach to learning; however, it draws upon selected practices of deductive learning. Our argument is not an indictment of deductive learning but, rather, a need to achieve balance between the two major approaches. Introducing inductive learning into the school is important for several reasons. First, schools should be enjoyable places that students want to attend rather than places they endure as part of their journey toward assimilation into the job market and the adult world. Second, schools should be places where students participate in and prepare for intelligent, creative, and effective living. This type of living includes learning how to analyze, criticize, and select from among alternative sources of information and courses of action; how to think effectively about unpredictable personal and interpersonal problems; how to live harmoniously with one another while remaining true to one's own emerging system of attitudes, beliefs, and values; and how to confront, clarify, and act upon problems and situations in constructive and creative ways. Finally, inductive learning is important because our society and democratic way of life are dependent upon an unlimited reservoir of creative and effective people. A small number of rare individuals have always emerged as the thinkers and problem solvers of our society. But we cannot afford to leave the emergence of leaders to chance, nor can we waste the undeveloped talents of so many of our young citizens who are the victims of poverty and the negative consequences that accompany being poor in America. All students must have the opportunity to develop their potentials and to lead constructive lives without trampling on or minimizing the value of others in the process.

Finally, returning to our previous chapter, we want to reiterate that the academic freedom and the opportunities for experimentation afforded programs for the gifted and talented have resulted in the kinds of enrichment learning and teaching we believe can be viable alternatives to the proliferation of didactic models that have been the centerpiece of most school reform initiatives. Gifted programs, even when they follow practices that are more restrictive than many people would like, are still the best experimental laboratories for total school improvement, and for this reason alone, it is curious why so many leaders in education are pursuing a vendetta that could lead to their demise.

Gifted Programs and the Bicycle Riders

People seeking to shout out their stand on the popular side of political correctness have turned gifted program bashing into a veritable cottage industry. It is always easy to attack the worst-case stereotypes of any practice, whether the practices be in business management, law enforcement, social welfare, or public education. Such attacks on worst-case scenarios are the centerpiece of George's chapter, and these worst-case scenarios have also acted as a target for other persons who are attempting to explain away educational initiatives that have not lived up to their expectations. Several examples can be found that illustrate how people have attempted to lay all the ills and woes of education at the feet of programs for the gifted. In *The Manufactured Crisis: Myths, Fraud, and Attack on America's Public Schools*, Berliner and Biddle (1995) jump on the bandwagon with a montage of almost bizarre reasons why gifted programs are a "poor idea." For example, they argue that because "Tchaikovsky's musical talents did not bloom until he was in his twenties... and the major contributions of Charles Darwin and Sigmund Freud did not begin to appear until those titans were in their forties" (p. 210), young persons should not be provided with enrichment and acceleration opportunities in school! These authors blatantly distort the summary chapter of Sternberg and Davidson's (1986) book entitled *Conceptions of Giftedness*, and they fall prey to the right-wing conspiracy argument that George presented in his chapter. Once again, we recommend that you not accept our interpretation of this work, but rather that you apply the me-as-researcher method by examining Berliner and Biddle's section about gifted programs (pp. 207-211), and then draw your own conclusions about the credibility of their work. We might ask you to remember, as you do this, that a recent federal report (U.S. Department of Education, 1993) called these very programs the laboratories of school improvement and further suggested that many current innovations in teaching had their roots in these programs.

A few months ago we were perusing a copy of *The School Administrator* (Goldman, 1996), and we ran across a news item entitled, "The

Movement's Forerunner Still Fighting for Nongradedness." The story is about Robert H. Anderson, a pioneer in the nongraded school movement, and his speculations about why this approach to school organization had not caught on. According to the article's author, "He [Anderson] thinks the conservative backlash to multiage grouping that some educators are experiencing is coming from parents and community members who do not understand the benefits, as well as parents of gifted children who do not want to lose their privileged status." It seems as though if anything is not working, we need a scapegoat, and what could be more convenient than good "ole" gifted programs.

We are reminded of a scene that took place in a film based on Katherine Ann Porter's (1945) landmark book entitled *Ship of Fools.* Herr Siegfried Rieber, newly enamored with the rise of Nazism in Germany, is pontificating about how all of Germany's troubles are the fault of the Jews. Karl Glocken replies, "Yes, yes, the Jews and the bicycle riders." "Why the bicycle riders?" asks Herr Rieber. "Why the Jews?" responds Glocken.

Perhaps, instead of placing all the blame for the growing dissatisfaction with our schools on programs for gifted students, we could end this response with a call for unity, creativity, and a commitment to work together to provide challenging, rewarding learning experiences for all students in our schools while simultaneously realizing that these learning experiences will never be the same for everyone. ■

References

Archambault, F. X., Westberg, K. L., Brown, S., Hallmark, B. W., Emmons, C., & Zhang, W. (1992). *Regular classroom practices with gifted students: Results of a national survey of classroom teachers* (Research Monograph No. 93102). Storrs, CT: The National Research Center on the Gifted and Talented.

Berliner, D. C., & Biddle, B. J. (1995). *The manufactured crisis: Myths, fraud and the attack on America's public schools.* Reading, MA: Addison-Wesley.

Carnegie Council on Adolescent Development. (1989). *Turning points: Preparing American youth for the 21st century.* New York: Carnegie Corporation.

Flanders, J. R. (1987). How much of the content in mathematics textbooks is new? *Arithmetic Teacher, 35,* 18-23.

Goldman, J. P. (1996). The movement's forerunner still fighting for nongradedness. *The School Administrator, 53* (1), 16.

Governor's School defended. (1995, November 22). *Education Week,* p. 12.

Kozol, J. (1991). *Savage inequities: Children in America's schools.* New York: Crown.

National Commission on Excellence in Education. (1983). *A nation at risk: The imperative of educational reform.* Report to the nation and the Secretary of Education. Washington, DC: U. S. Government Printing Office.

Porter, K. A. (1945). *Ship of fools.* Boston: Little Brown and Company.

Reis, S. M., Westberg, K. L., Kulikowich, J., Caillard, F., Hébert, T., Plucker, J., Purcell, J. H., Rogers, J. B., & Smist, J. M. (1993). *Why not let high ability students start school in January? The curriculum compacting study.* Storrs, CT: The National Research Center on the Gifted and Talented.

Renzulli, J. S. (1973). *Talented potential in minority group students.* The First National Conference on the Disadvantaged Gifted. Ventura, CA: Ventura County Superintendent of Schools.

Renzulli, J. S. (1978). What makes giftedness? Reexamining a definition. *Phi Delta Kappan, 60* (5), 180-184.

Sternberg, R. J., & Davidson, J. E. (Eds.). (1986). *Conceptions of giftedness.* New York: Cambridge University Press.

Taylor, B. M., & Frye, B. J. (1988). Pretesting: Minimize time spent on skill work for intermediate readers. *The Reading Teacher, 42* (2), 100-103.

U.S. Department of Education (1993). National excellence: A case for developing America's talent. Washington, DC: U.S. Goverment Printing Office.

Usiskin, Z. (1987). Why elementary algebra can, should, and must be an eighth-grade course for average students. *Mathematics Teacher, 80,* 428-438.

Vonnegut, K. (1968). *Welcome to the monkey house.* New York: Dell Publishing.

Westberg, K. L., Archambault, F. X., Dobyns, S. M., & Salvin, T. J. (1992). *Technical report: An observational study of instructional and curricular practices used with gifted and talented students in regular classrooms.* Storrs, CT: The National Research Center on the Gifted and Talented.

The authors would like to thank Karen Kettle for valuable assistance in the preparation of this chapter. Research for this chapter was supported under the Javits Act Program (Grant No. R206R50001) as administered by the Office of Educational Research and Improvement, U.S. Department of Education. The findings and opinions expressed in this chapter do not reflect the position or policies of the National Institute on the Education of At-Risk Students, the Office of Educational Research and Improvement, or the U.S. Department of Education.

VI

Challenging Students to Develop Their Talents

Thomas O. Erb

In reading the preceding four chapters, I detect much upon which Professor George agrees with Professors Renzulli and Reis. I see a basis for moving forward to challenge middle school youngsters to develop their talents as part of a balanced effort to promote healthy growth. Though there is a basis for advancing the cause of talent development within the context of a diversified middle school, there are demons out there that continue to threaten both general middle grades education and the effort to promote gifted performances among young adolescents.

Some demons still dog us

Reading George then Renzulli and Reis reveals demons on both sides of the issue. It appears that both middle schools and education for giftedness suffer by both being unfairly bashed, on the one hand, and being used to promote questionable ends on the other. Middle schools are criticized for fostering a "one-size-fits-all" curriculum that fights excellence by promoting mediocrity and sacrificing talent development on the altar of "democracy." Middle school promoters are accused of creating holding pens for youth to encourage their social-emotional growth at the expense of their cognitive development. Some middle school advocates reinforce this perception by focusing on stereotypes about plateaued brain growth and raging hormones that project an unflattering picture of young adolescents.

For their part, gifted programs get bashed in order to cover up bigger failures in school reform. Programs for the gifted may be among the first to go if the test scores stay low. There are calls to cut the "frills," such as programs for the gifted, to raise the "bottom line." Many programs for the gifted are especially vulnerable to these calls because they are disproportionately populated with middle class majority children as opposed to minority students or those more at risk. To complicate the criticism that gifted programs take, some patrons use these programs to promote illegitimate ends such as resegregating public schools from within. With a historical overlap between the identification of "giftedness" and the condition of "middle-class-whiteness," some people are not above exploiting this reality to maintain racial and social class barriers in otherwise "public" schools, all in the name, of course, of promoting learning by letting students learn among others "with similar needs."

Some political forces simultaneously threaten both middle schools and the approach to gifted education advocated by Renzulli and Reis. Kohn (1998) has clearly outlined how local elites thwart school reform precisely because it does promise to be more inclusionary and address diverse learner needs. The agenda of these elites is not to promote the education of a new generation, but instead to make sure that their own children get a competitive advantage from the unequal allocation of scarce public school resources.

This drama has been playing out recently in Howard County, Maryland (Bradley, 1998). There local elites have bashed the middle schools which contain some of the most progressive gifted programs in the country based on the Schoolwide Enrichment Model (Erb, Gibson, & Aubin, 1995). Specifically under attack are "exploratory" classes and "heterogeneous" classes. The solution according to the middle school critics is a return to tracking. Interestingly enough, and perhaps not coincidentally, the push to create divisions among students in the schools of Howard County is accompanied by a simultaneous resegregation of Columbia, Maryland (Biggar, 1998). Columbia, designed to be a racially and economically diverse community midway between Washington and Baltimore, is moving away from racial integration. As Biggar put it: "As Columbians socialize less across racial lines, they understand each other less, increasing the possibility for racial tension." The move to push this community condition into the schools poses a threat not only to middle schools dedicated to educating all students but also to the approaches to talent development that Renzulli and Reis have articulated in this volume. It is within this sociopolitical context that educators will attempt to deliver programs based on the educational needs of students.

What the writing of each of our authors has brought to light is that the issues related to talent development in the middle grades are being played out in both the professional and political arenas. The crafting of programs to meet the needs of high achieving children will take place in the context of not only professionals attempting to render judgments on one level, but also parents, legislators, and school board members exercising their power and influence to constrain the parameters within which educators operate. Recognizing that educators will not have full reign to exercise their best judgment about how to promote talent development in the middle grades, we shall, nevertheless, focus on the curricular and instructional aspects of the dilemma.

I choose this focus for three reasons. First, the audience for this book is intended to be primarily educators who are responsible for curricular and instructional decisions. Second, the writers in this book, including the author of this chapter, have stronger backgrounds in curricular and instructional issues than in administrative or political ones. Finally, this book is part of a continuing dialogue aimed at controlling the internecine conflict among educators regarding addressing diverse learning needs among young adolescents. Consequently, focusing on matters over which educators do have influence should be more productive in moving the professional, as opposed to political, discussion forward. For if educators cannot reach some common understanding and agreement about the role of middle schools in talent development, then dealing with the external pressures will remain very difficult indeed.

There is a solid platform from which to go forward

In the realm of curriculum and instruction, George and Renzulli and Reis have found several elements upon which they agree. I have drawn these conclusions from direct statements that they have written as well as from inferences I have opined from reading their responses to each other. These conclusions are not necessarily discussed in order of their importance – that is for the reader to decide. However, I have intended that there be some order to their placement. The conclusions that follow begin with a focus on the current state of affairs, proceed through issues related to identification and participation, and end with a focus on programmatic solutions to the problem of promoting talent development.

1. **Current practice does not deal well with diversity.** Too many students with all kinds of learning styles and talents are unchallenged and bored in middle grades classrooms. Too many students with various backgrounds and abilities remain unengaged while their learning needs are unmet. Educators need to do a better job of meeting the instructional needs of these various types of learners. There needs to be more instructional variety, more opportunity for individual and small group projects, more collaboration among teachers, and more chance to create real-world products once basic skills are demonstrated.

2. **Identification of those who can benefit from services for the gifted needs to be inclusive, not exclusive.** All sides agree that tracking students into "gifted" classes based on test scores is dysfunctional. Instead, opportunities to pursue gifted performances should be open to all students who wish to engage in those efforts. Teachers should help match students to these opportunities by looking for signs of talent in student products, by exposing students to a variety of experiences to stimulate their curiosity, and by encouraging students to pursue their personal interests beyond minimal expectations. By focusing on excellence in student performance, as opposed to labeling some subset of

180

students as the "gifted" ones, educators can help to create an atmosphere where talented performance is respected by a wide range of students, rather than class membership being a status symbol the divides students from one another.

3. **Class and racial barriers that prevent participation in talent development activities need to be eliminated.** Quite the contrary to using gifted programs to resegregate schools, not only should opportunities to pursue gifted performances be open and available, but also participation in learning activities should reflect the ethnic and social class diversity of the school. If special accommodations are necessary to allow the participation of some students whose education backgrounds are deficient, then they should be provided. While there may be little that schools can do to ameliorate the social and economic problems of the larger society, they can at least work within the school to remove class and racial barriers to full participation in appropriate learning activities.

4. **The Schoolwide Enrichment Model offers a promising path for encouraging talent development.** The Schoolwide Enrichment Model is compatible with the middle school concept and can work in the context of heterogeneous, interdisciplinary teams. The model provides for all students to be exposed to stimulating activities and events aimed at peaking their interest.

5. **"Enrichment clusters" fit well with middle school curricular options.** Clubs, minicourses, and special interest activities have long been a part of the middle school concept (George & Alexander, 1993; Lounsbury & Vars, 1978). These are designed to allow students to pursue personal interests, many of which are extensions of core or exploratory courses. Several times a year, these offerings permit students to make choices about what activity to engage in next. The enrichment cluster concept fits well with the idea of clubs or minicourses in which faculty members or even community volunteers assist students' creating real-world products or preparing for some type of public performance.

6. **Teacher collaboration will lead to students' needs being better met.** All authors would welcome more teachers' working together to provide learning experiences for students. The interdisciplinary team should consist of not only subject specialists, but also resource teachers of the gifted. These resource teachers can help regular classroom teachers plan and execute enrichment activities, identify students' needs, acquire special resources, make curriculum adaptations, and plan enrichment clusters. A number of issues related to addressing student needs in the context of interdisciplinary teaming are explored in Dickinson and Erb (1997). The old notion that subject specialists working alone or teachers of the gifted working independently can meet students' diverse learning needs is no longer viable. Teamwork is required to determine student needs and then design, facilitate, and assess learning activities.

7. **Integrated curriculum can be a useful vehicle for balancing deductive and inductive learning strategies.** The notion that learning occurs in different phases is not new. Earlier in this century, Whitehead (1963) described a learning cycle consisting of "romance," "precision," and "generalization." These three stages were described recently by an Olympic skating coach as "discovering," "mastering," and "creating." These stages of learning parallel the three types of learning activities that characterize the Schoolwide Enrichment Model. Type I activities focus on discovering, Type II on mastering, and Type III on creating. Furthermore, according to Erb and Doda (1989), these three stages are also the foundation of effective thematic unit planning. The precision or mastering stage is based on deductive learning while the romance or discovering stage and the generalization or creating stage require an emphasis on inductive learning. It appears that the curricular models being advocated for high achievers and some curriculum integration models being advocated for all middle school learners have similar pedagogical foundations.

These seven elements provide a sound basis from which to plan for talent development within the framework of a middle school designed around heterogeneous, interdisciplinary teams. The small learning community, which is the team, combined with other components of the middle school concept provide a varied and flexible format within which to meet a wide range of student needs, including those of students who need extra challenges in academic areas.

Balancing community with the development of individuals

The middle school concept is designed to make two seemingly contradictory goals compatible. One is to provide a common core curriculum to all future citizens of our democracy. The other is to meet each child on his or her own level in order to provide developmentally appropriate instruction. Essential as these two opposing concepts are to the success of a good middle school, taken to their logical extremes neither notion makes sense. If common core means every student should be treated equally, then an absurd curriculum would result where few students in a diverse population would find an appropriate level of challenge. If, on the other hand, every child is unique so that he or she cannot be educated without an individual educational plan (IEP), what happens to the idea that any set of common experiences, knowledge, skills, and attitudes binds us together into community?

Clearly some dynamic tension between common core and individual development must play itself out in our middle level schools. There must be common experiences, understandings, and causes that build community spirit and allow students to identify with things that are bigger than themselves. At the same time they need to identify their unique selves and develop their individual talents to the fullest.

We can point to many activities associated with schools and society generally that combine these opposing elements. One of the most obvious is team sports. Participants play the same game with a common set of rules. However, each individual plays a different role and more is expected of some players than others. Not every basketball, football, volleyball, or soccer player has the same level of talent. Yet, different students work to develop their own skills and talents to the highest level possible out of a personal desire to excel. At the same time the team's success is dependent on these individual differences. All of these sports require that different positions be played well on both defense and offense. The team's success is *not* dependent on having star individuals working in isolation, but instead is contingent upon different talents working together.

Some team sports are a blend of individual development and community building in yet another way. The communality of spectator sports played by individuals of differing talents is further illustrated by the community spirit they engender that transcends membership on the team.

Most musical groups are also examples that demonstrate the blending of individual talent development with building a sense of belonging to something bigger than oneself. Choirs, bands, and orchestras provide the opportunity for individuals to develop talent in various capacities. Though all participants have an opportunity to contribute, some preform at higher levels than others. There are first chairs and concert masters. However, the success of the group is not determined alone by how well the best preform; but, perhaps more importantly, by how well the least talented perform! Yet, the score – the curriculum – is the same for all. Though each student is playing a separate instrument, the whole orchestra is playing the same tune. How absurd it would be for the violinists to insist that they only play certain songs while the brass section resists because the songs that show off the talents of the violinists are not the most challenging for their section. While the whole orchestra is on the same page of the same score, individuals are contributing in their unique ways to the success of the whole. Once again, regardless of one's own individual accomplishments, being part of a valued group is significant in its own right.

Moving our perspective into the academic classroom, we can find the same blend of common curriculum and individual accommodation. An entire interdisciplinary team is studying a thematic unit entitled

"Survival" (Slyter, Etheridge, Umbarger, & Roberts, 1993). Integrating objectives for this unit include the following:

The students will. . .

1. Develop group organizational skills related to choosing leadership and defining and delegating group tasks.

2. Develop group problem solving skills such as defining the problem, identifying resources to help solve the problem, and proposing a solution to the problem.

3. Develop research skills such as using the library, locating resources on the Internet, and recording data.

4. Develop skills in decision making by planning an expedition and presenting the plan to an audience.

5. Demonstrate an understanding of how competition might be both beneficial and harmful in a group situation.

6. Demonstrate an understanding of how cooperation might be both beneficial and harmful in a group situation.

All students are introduced to this "Survival" unit through a trip to a local "challenge course." After experiencing the course, students discuss the respective roles of cooperation and competition in the successful completion of that course. For the next several weeks the students study curricular content in social studies, mathematics, language arts, and science to acquire the skills and knowledge needed to complete the culminating activities for the unit. Working in small cooperative groups, the students are to create an Adventurer's Guide Packet for the trip of their choice. The choices are these:

1. Sailing down the Amazon
2. Survival at the South Pole
3. Westward Ho!
4. Search for Tut's Tomb
5. Where Is Dr. Livingston?: A Tropical Rain Forest Adventure
6. Scaling Mt. Everest
7. Discovering Atlantis: A Deep Sea Adventure
8. Race to the North Pole

Students are to create adventure packets that show what they have learned in each of their core classes. The following elements are to be imaginatively included in the final project:

1. Description of the environment
2. Purpose of the expedition
3. Expected dangers: Emphasizing "Man vs. Nature" relationship
4. Total distance to be traveled
5. Distance to be traveled per day
6. Length of journey
7. Foods taken
8. Average pack weight
9. Cultural traditions of the area
10. Historical significance of the expedition
11. Geographical challenges that face the expedition
12. Simulated journal of participant on the expedition
13. Paragraphs describing effects of cooperation and competition
14. Visual aids

All students are held accountable for the same curricular objectives in social studies, mathematics, science, and language arts as well as for the unifying objectives listed above. All students are introduced to this unit with the same activity: the trip to the challenge course. However, there are plenty of opportunities built into the unit for individual talents to be expressed. In the first place students have some choice about which "trip" they would plan in order to meet the objectives of the unit. Within these groups there are opportunities for students to do some division of labor or specialization – allowing students with artistic talent, drama talent, writing talent, or math talent to make exceptional contributions to their projects. Finally, since each group is creating a unique product, there is built into the unit the opportunity for students to choose the level to which they would perform in creating their "Adventurer's Guides." As does playing a basketball game or performing a musical number, the integrated thematic unit described here is based on common curricular objectives, but is designed to require unique contributions from the various participants who are not all performing at the same level of ability.

Using curriculum to the fullest

If the middle school concept is fully understood, then middle schools in practice should be able to accommodate diversity, including giftedness in its various manifestations. The curriculum of a fully developed middle school provides for young adolescents to participate in a common core curriculum that encompasses the history, language, music, literature, geography, art, natural science, health, technology, mathematics, and life skills that all Americans need to hold in common. In addition to the common core, which includes such required exploratory classes as art, foreign languages, technology, and practical arts, the middle school curriculum provides for elective classes that students can take to go beyond the basic expectations. These vary from place to place but usually include formal foreign language study, various classes in art, drama, music, vocational/technical skills, and journalism.

Beyond core and elective classes, the middle school curriculum provides for a wide variety of student activities. These activities constitute a broad smorgasbord that is open for all students to choose from. However, that does not mean that all activities are necessarily appropriate for all students. It is in the activities program that a multitude of changing student interests, talents, and abilities can be accommodated. Activities/clubs/minicourses differ from core and elective classes in that they last for shorter periods of time – typically four, six, or nine weeks. Then students choose other options so that they experience a variety of short-term special interest activities. A complete program will offer students choices in every one of Gardner's multiple intelligences plus a variety of special interests. Such a program will offer academic extensions in literature and drama, sciences, social studies, mathematics, and foreign languages. In addition, offerings will be made in the following categories:

- arts & crafts
- physical fitness & games

187

- personal development/health
- communications (of various types)
- service activities
- board games & logical puzzles
- musical options
- leisure & recreational activities

Among these offerings that are open to everyone should be options that will interest students in a variety of advanced activities: math counts; history day; odyssey of the mind; science fair; preparation for drama, music, and debate competitions; as well as creative writing; book club; creative drama; specialized music performance; and integrative activities such as film making, video production, and computer applications.

Finally, the middle school curriculum calls for an advisory time for students to examine their interests and talents, set goals, and match their interests to the opportunities available in the middle school. Rapidly developing young adolescents, of whatever abilities and interests, need adult guidance to relate their emerging talents to the opportunities available at school and in their communities. Helping students make choices about what activities, clubs, or minicourses to choose is a proper advisory function. This process requires that students examine themselves and assess the opportunities available to them. This process of making choices should include not only help from an advisor but communication with parents as well. This is an excellent opportunity for parents and students to talk with each other about what challenges to undertake, which ones to put on hold, and which ones to avoid. For many young adolescents, this process is one of setting priorities, making decisions, and sticking by those decisions for a short period of time. Then a new cycle of making choices begins.

Another advisory function is helping students monitor their experiences in school. If, for example, a student professes to be bored in a class, it is a proper advisory function to help the student analyze the causes of that situation so that solutions can be proposed. If such a perception of circumstances exists, advisors can help students figure out what they, as students, can do about the situation. Questions such as, "Are you taking full advantage of the opportunities that already exist at school?" can be asked. Perhaps adjustments can be negotiated that will provide more challenging opportunities for students. This is an example of the advocacy role in the advisory function.

Some might argue that a student should not have to go through all of this to have his or her needs met. However, testing children and placing them in special classes does not guarantee that their needs would be met either. Where teachers assume homogeneity in a class, they may be even less sensitive to accommodating individual differences than a teacher who makes no such assumption to begin with. In short, there is no way to guarantee that young adolescents' needs, diverse as they are, are going to be met in whatever learning arrangement we place them. Therefore, it is always important to provide the time for students, with the help of a caring adults, to reflect on their learning experiences and take action to improve what they can.

In summary, if educators implement a varied curriculum and help students take full advantage of the options provided, a wide variety of student needs can be accommodated. This process starts within the common core. Students need to exercise choices of how to meet objectives through individual and small group projects tied to the basic curriculum. Beyond the core which includes required exploratory classes, middle schools need to provide as many elective options as local resources will allow. In addition, a complete curriculum allows students to choose from a variety of activities, clubs, and minicourses. In each case, these options should allow students with special interests and talents to go beyond the basics. Finally, students must be helped to take full advantage of these options through the last essential curricular element: the advisory program. The advisory program is the clearing house that helps students take full personal advantage of the learning opportunities available.

A middle school is a liberating organization: Free yourselves

Not only will a well-designed curriculum meet the needs of a wide variety of learners, both those with special needs as well as those with

189

special talents (many of whom are the same students), but the organizational design of a true middle school provides flexibility not found in factory-model junior high schools. When it is argued that individual teachers cannot meet the needs of diverse learners in their heterogeneous classes, it is easy to sympathize. But it is also necessary to point out that true middle schools do not ask teachers to solve these problems alone as they are asked to do in departmentalized junior highs.

Middle schools are built around the notion that teaching is too complex to be left to individuals abandoned to fend for themselves. That is why the interdisciplinary team was designed (see Dickinson & Erb, 1997). When teachers share students whose learning they are jointly responsible for, plan together, share a common area of the building, and have a flexible block teaching schedule to work with, they can do things with each other, with other professionals, with students, with instruction, and with the curriculum that are either impossible or much more difficult in departmentalized schools. I have never encountered a group of teachers who, when asked to brainstorm for fifteen minutes, failed to generate 15 to 30 things that teachers can control in a teamed situation that are beyond their control in a departmentalized school.

Teamed middle schools provide teachers with a great deal of control over the variables that affect learning. With a flexible block schedule, the uniform periods of equal length that are imposed in departmentalized organizations are not a requirement unless teachers choose them. Time for labs, special projects, extra help, longer group assignments, or shorter encounters are all controllable by teachers.

One of the biggest advantages for teamed teachers is to control the instructional groups that students are assigned to. However, here is where middle school "ideology" can get in the way to blind teachers to the choices that they can exercise. An interdisciplinary team is not an instructional group. A heterogeneous team is not incompatible with various types of homogeneous instructional groups. The interdisciplinary team is a learning community of 75 to 150 students. This community should reflect the diversity present in the local community. Therefore, each team should contain about the same demographic diversity that is found in the general school population.

However, it does not follow that students with similar learning needs should never be grouped together for instruction. Though it may make very good pedagogical sense to group together a high ability student with a couple of average ability and one who is of lower ability, using this arrangement exclusively as an organizing principle for cooperative learning groups is a reflection of the very rigidity that middle schools are supposed to be overcoming, not perpetuating. While these types of groups are one manifestation of the use of flexible groups within a team, they are not the only one. Why not create groups of students with similar levels of performance to learn new skills. Do some students not need more teacher assistance to learn a skill than do others? The key is that learning groups within the team are subject to regrouping when a new skill or other curricular objective is being pursued. In the interdisciplinary thematic unit discussed above the project groups are one type of flexible learning group. Within that same unit students could be regrouped to learn the mathematics skills needed to carry out the culminating activities, the creation of the Adventurer's Guides. Students would be regrouped into different learning groups within the other subject areas taught by the team. To get a better understanding of how classrooms can be managed to accommodate student diversity see Kierstead (1985, 1986).

In this discussion the existence of a team is always assumed. It is much harder to make this flexible grouping work in isolated classrooms. Because teachers on teams meet regularly they mentor each other in ways that seldom occur in departmentalized schools (Powell & Mills, 1994). Teams bring more to bear on solving instructional problems – multiple perspectives coupled with a wider array of talent and skill – than is usually available to the isolated subject specialist.

From the perspective of the middle school concept, there is no reason to not have grouped classes within a heterogeneous team. Students can be grouped for various levels of instruction in math and heterogeneously regrouped for instruction in other subjects taught by the team. When teachers control the grouping within their own teams, as Dunning (1988; Erb & Doda, 1989) and Nolan (1998) have shown how to do, they are demonstrating flexible decision making in creating learning groups. Just because heterogeneous teams are desirable, does not make it easy to continue to maintain that students should be restricted from having instruction at their appropriate levels. But what we can now do is to provide alternatives to accommodate most of this diversity within a heterogeneous team. This is not accomplished by teaching "eighth grade math" to all students, but by grouping within the team and then further grouping within classes. And in the end there may be some students who will need to have their needs negotiated on a case-by-case basis to be met beyond the limits of the team.

Finally, this discussion of the flexibility of the team assumes that services are brought to the students on the team. Various learning specialists, either as full members or as frequent consultants, will plan with the subject specialists on the team to provide differentiated learning opportunities. These can be provided in the context of interdisciplinary units as illustrated above or within subject area instructional activities. There is much more power in the organizational arrangements of middle schools than many of its advocates have manifested to date.

Certainly, pursuing the organizational and curricular flexibilities of the middle school provides a much better path for meeting individual needs than resorting to the departmentalized rigidities and preselected learning groups of factory-model schools. By digesting, debating, and negotiating the ideas of Paul George, Joe Renzulli, and Sally Reis we should be in a better position to exploit the power of the middle school to accommodate student diversity without fragmenting community. ■

References
Biggar, V. (1998, April 27). Do planned communities work? *Morning edition.* Washington, DC: National Public Radio, Inc. (Transcribed by Federal Document Clearing House, Inc.)

Bradley, A. (1998, April 15). Muddle in the middle. *Education Week, 17*(31), 38-42.

Dickinson, T. S., & Erb, T. O. (Eds.). (1997). *We gain more than we give: Teaming in middle schools.* Columbus, OH: National Middle School Association.

Dunning, E. A. (1988). Harmony vs. discord. *The NELMS Journal, 1* (2), 23-26.

Erb, T. O., & Doda, N. M. (1989). *Team organization: Promise—practices and possibilities.* Washington, DC: National Education Association.

Erb, T.O., Gibson, S., & Aubin, S. (1995). Promoting gifted behavior in an untracted middle school setting. In B. Pool & J. Page (Eds.), *Beyond tracking: Finding success in inclusive schools* (pp. 133-140). Bloomington, IN: Phi Delta Kappa.

George, P. S., & Alexander, W. M. (1993). *The exemplary middle school* (2nd ed.). Fort Worth, TX: Harcourt Brace Jovanovich College Publishers.

Kierstead, J. (1985). Direct instruction and experiential approaches: Are they mutually exclusive? *Educational Leadership, 42* (8), 25-30.

Kierstead, J. (1986). How teachers manage individual and small group work in active classrooms. *Educational Leadership, 44* (2), 22-25.

Kohn, A. (1998). Only for *my* kid: How privileged parents undermine school reform. *Phi Delta Kappan, 79,* 569-577.

Lounsbury, J. H., & Vars, G. F. (1978). *A curriculum for the middle school years.* New York: Harper and Row.

Nolan, F. (1998). Ability grouping plus heterogeneous grouping: Win-win schedules. *Middle School Journal, 29* (5), 14-19.

Powell, R. R., & Mills, R. (1994). Five types of mentoring build knowledge on interdisciplinary teams. *Middle School Journal, 26* (2), 24-30.

Slyter, K., Etheridge, S., Umbarger, B., & Roberts, S. (1993). *Survival: A unit in cooperation and competition.* Unpublished interdisciplinary thematic unit.

Whitehead, A. N. (1963). *The aims of education.* New York: Mentor Books.

National Middle School Association

National Middle School Association was established in 1973 to serve as a voice for professionals and others interested in the education of young adolescents. The Association has grown rapidly and now enrolls members in all fifty states, the Canadian provinces, and forty-two other nations. In addition, fifty-six state, regional, and provincial middle school associations are official affiliates of NMSA.

NMSA is the only association dedicated exclusively to the education, development, and growth of young adolescents. Membership is open to all. While middle level teachers and administrators make up the bulk of the membership, central office personnel, college and university faculty, state department officials, other professionals, parents, and lay citizens are members and active in supporting our single mission – improving the educational experiences of 10-15 year olds. This open and diverse membership is a particular strength of NMSA.

The Association provides a variety of services, conferences, and materials in fulfilling its mission. The association publishes *Middle School Journal*, the movement's premier professional journal; *Research in Middle Level Education Quarterly; Middle Ground, the Magazine of Middle Level Education; Target*, the association's newsletter; and *The Family Connection*, a newsletter for families. In addition, the association publishes more than fifty books and monographs on all aspects of middle level education. The Association's highly acclaimed annual conference, which has drawn approximately 10,000 registrants in recent years, is held in the fall.

For information about NMSA and its many services contact the Headquarters at 2600 Corporate Exchange Drive, Suite 370, Columbus, Ohio 43231, TELEPHONE: 800-528-NMSA; FAX: 614-895-4750; WWW. NMSA.ORG.